INSIGHT POCK

Gran Canaria

APA PUBLICATIONS
Part of the Langenscheidt Publishing Group
L

The Canary Islands

Welcome!

Known by the ancient Greeks as the 'makaron nesoi' (Fortunate Islands) and by the Romans as the Land of Eternal Spring, the Canary Islands have always seemed to exist more in myth than in reality. Though Spanish, they lie 100km (62 miles) adrift from the coast of Africa, some 1,000km (620 miles) from Spain. The most diverse of the islands is Gran Canaria, the subject of this guide. While people bask in the sun at Playa del Inglés, its most popular resort, snow can cap the peaks at Tejeda, 40km (25 miles) inland.

In these pages, Insight's corespondent on Gran Canaria, Margaret Hart, has devised a series of itineraries linking the island's highlights: the first seven are devoted to Las Palmas and the north and the remaining four concentrate on the attractions of the south, taking the resort of Playa del Inglés as a base. Supporting the itineraries are sections on history and culture, shopping, eating out and nightlife, as well as a calendar of special events and a practical information section providing vital tips.

Margaret Hart has lived in Gran Canaria for around 15 years, earning her living as an interpreter and lecturer in tourism. In this guide her aim is to reveal the less publicised attractions of Gran Canaria, which even committed sunseekers come to admire most – if only they are introduced. She hopes to prise visitors off the island's sand and send them in search of its soul. That said, she has not neglected the justly famous beaches, which have been child-tested by her own two girls.

C O N T E N T S

History & Culture

Las Palmas & the North

Seven itineraries take you to the highlights of the north, from a day exploring the capital Las Palmas (Itinerary 1) to a roller coaster ride to the island's highest point (Itinerary 3). The first three itineraries in this section are designed as full-day tours, the remaining four as half-day options.

Pages 2/3: Puerto de las Nieves

The South

The remaining itineraries in the guide are devoted to the south of Gran Canaria, where most of the main beach resorts are found. They use Playa del Inglés/Maspalomas as a base.

Shopping, Eating Out & Nightlife

Calendar of Special Events

Practical Information

Maps

Pages 8/9: camel safari in the south

HISTORY & CULTURE

It is always difficult to separate the myth from the reality in the history and culture of the Canary Islands. Nobody is really clear what the Canary Islands were like before the 14th century, when the Spanish invaders finally put them on the geographical map and wiped the original Guanche culture off the face of the earth. If legend is anything to go by, Gran Canaria and its sister islands appear to have been a kind of pastoral Arcadia. Both the Greeks and Romans wrote about them in glowing terms, calling them the Hesperides, the Gardens of the Gods and Land of Eternal Spring and thereby, somewhat unwittingly, setting them firmly on their way to becoming the great tourist attractions they are today.

Nor are the geological origins of the islands free from mythical interpretations. For many, the islands represent the remains of the sunken continent of Atlantis. A slightly more scientific hypothesis maintains that they are parts of Africa which broke away and drifted

Myths – such as the tree which showered water – make up Canarian history

like ice floes in the shifting and sliding of the continents. The most extravagant of the hypotheses goes so far as to claim that the islands are the summits of a mountain chain which is still nosing its way upwards out of the Atlantic Ocean. What is known for certain is that they are volcanic islands, some of which are over 10 million years old.

Origins

The name 'Canary Islands' calls to mind the yellow song birds we like to keep in cages – but don't expect to find canaries fluttering around here. There are all sorts of theories on the origin of the name of the islands, but song birds don't feature in any of them. The most commonly held theory is recorded by Pliny in his account of an exploratory expedition sent by King Juba II of Mauretania to the island of Gran Canaria. The expedition returned to Mauretania with two large dogs, the *canes* of Canaria. That the locals share this theory is apparent in their coat-of-arms, emblazoned with two dogs, and the bronze sculptures of dogs that grace the Plaza de Santa Ana in Las Palmas (*see Itinerary 1, page 22*).

Dogs gave the islands their name

However, there are no such doubts as to the origins of the 'Gran' in Gran Canaria. The heroic and stubborn defence of the island led the Spanish invaders to christen it 'Great'. For a long time, the Spaniards struggled to conquer the island, their difficulty largely due to the 14 local chieftains, the *guanartemes*, who rallied together together to stave off the enemy attacks. On the other Canary Islands the leaders were divided among themselves, making the Spaniards' job much easier. Again, if legend is to be believed, the unity encountered on Gran Canaria was the work of Princess Andamana of Gáldar, a woman of potent charm who seduced all 14 chieftains, thereby giving them something in common to fight for, and then married her blood brother to avoid causing rifts between her former suitors. On the other islands, in contrast, the women tended to fall prey to the Spaniards' charms and helped them in their conquest – particularly on El Hierro, the smallest of the Canary Islands.

Gran Canaria also fares favourably in etymological comparisons with the other islands, especially with Tenerife, which was originally known as Hell, possibly because Teide, the island's highest mountain, was then an active volcano.

Death of a Culture

Faced with the inevitability of defeat by the Spanish, the *guanartemes* on Gran Canaria decided to end it all rather than live in slavery. Their method of death was as drastic as it was spectacular: they threw themselves off the highest rockfaces of the island. Those who survived the invasion quickly adapted to their new circumstances. The Guanches were, after all, a peace-loving, law-abiding race of cave-dwellers who divided their time between their communal fields and their herds of goats. Their two games of skill which were at all warlike in nature – the *juego del garrote* (two opponents armed with shepherds' crooks) and the *lucha canaria* (a kind of wrestling match) were only played to pass the time when they were not singing or dancing.

Their God was *Alcorán*, the God of the Sky, and their religion was based on fertility rites and rainmaking ceremonies. The two sacred mountains of Humiaga (now Cuatro Puertas: see *Itineraries*) and Tirma were used as *harimaguadas*, sanctuaries for the virgin daughters of their nobility. Before being married off, these girls were taken to special grain stores, such as the Cenobio de Valerón, to be fattened for the event. These young women were highly important in the Guanche culture since it was through them that the race was perpetuated. According to legend, in Gomera and Gran Canaria it was customary for a man to 'gift' his wife to a visiting guest in order to introduce new blood into the family.

The Spanish invaders described the Guanche men as exceedingly tall and the women as incredibly beautiful. Though it should be remembered that the average Spaniard of the time was no giant and that the soldiers had been a long time at sea without clapping eyes on a woman, the evidence does actually indicate that the Spaniards might have been right: mummies on display in the Museo Canario in Las Palmas are around 1.84m (6ft) tall, certainly way above the average of the time.

A Guanche mummy

The process of mummification was elaborate. It involved disembowelling the corpse, bathing it in shallow salt water (the Guanches apparently did not swim), then leaving it to dry, after which the body was wrapped in goatskins and buried in one of a number of ways, depending upon social rank. The sap of the *drago*, the dragon tree indigenous to the islands, seems to have played an essential part in this ritual. Called 'dragon's blood' on account of its reddish colour, the sap was held to possess miraculous healing properties – which is probably just as well since the Guanches' other important form of medical treatment was *trepanación* – a hole in the head.

The Spaniards brought Christianity

Roots and Politics

To all intents and purposes, the culture of the Guanches disappeared after the Conquest and the subsequent incorporation of the island into the Spanish kingdom of the Catholic Monarchs, Ferdinand and Isabella, in 1478. Unfortunately there were no written records of the original language, which is thought to have been of Berber (African) origin. Canary Spanish is very different from mainland Spanish but this is only to be expected of islands which are nearer Africa than Spain and have received influxes of people from all parts of the world. Moreover many Canarios who migrated to various parts of Latin America, above all Venezuela and Cuba, later returned to their beloved islands with new words and phrases. Words such as *naife* (knife) or *guagua* (bus) only exist here, so even mainland Spaniards sometimes have trouble understanding the islanders.

Short-lived attempts have been made to dig out cultural roots and restore the lost Guanche identity, mainly by artists and intellectuals. The most important work has been done by the Millares family, above all the painter Manolo Millares. Other influential figures include the sculptor Martin Chirino, who has incorporated the symbols of the *pintaderas* (the wooden or terracotta seals of the Guanches) into his work; Tony Gallardo, who works mainly with volcanic rock; the Padorno brothers; and the outspoken lady artist, Lola Massien.

Political movements of a nationalistic nature have only recently become popular on the island. Up until the beginning of the 1990s, the people of Gran Canaria, in particular, had tended to be middle-of-the-road in their politics. Indeed, the only seat won by the Central Democratic Pary in the whole of Spain in elections in 1990 was in Gran Canaria. In the early 1970s there was a spate of bomb

Typical dress in the 1830s

scares mainly stage-managed by the lawyer Antonio Cubillo and his radically nationalistic political party, MPAIAC. Exiled at the time in Algeria, Cubillo used to broadcast political propaganda over the radio and became an almost mythical figure. But democracy has changed all that and Cubillo is now considered an anecdotal and picturesque figure from the past.

However, the traditional rivalry between the two major islands of Gran Canaria and Tenerife, the latter presently ruled by a virulently insular party, has led to greater interest in local parties, although Gran Canaria always opts for the major national parties when it comes to the crunch.

A Bridge Between Continents

The Canary Islands have long been important as a strategic port of call. Columbus stopped off here at least once en route to America. The strong trading links which were established between the Canary Islands, Europe, America and Africa were to bring people of all nations to these shores. At the time when sugar cultivation was booming in the south of the island (at Agüimes and Ingenio, for example) slaves were brought here, mainly by the Portuguese, from Africa. Thus, in Gran Canaria, there are two distinctly different strains of people: the tall, slender fair-skinned Canary islanders (the original Guanches were said to be redheads) and the swarthy, dark-skinned wiry-haired mainlanders. Although the ancient custom of gifting the wife no longer exists, the introduction of 'new blood' by people from all parts of the world is apparent – above all on islands such as Fuerteventura where blonde-haired locals were non-existent before tourism.

Columbus is remembered here

Hotel patio from the early days of tourism

The first and most important settlers were the British who originally came for reasons of health. One of the first tourist guides was Samler Brown's *Madeira, Canary Islands and Azores: A Practical and Complete Guide for the use of Tourists and Invalids* published in 1898. The British are held in great esteem by the Gran Canarians because their presence on the island has proved highly beneficial. For a long time Britain was the main foreign market for the principal exports from Gran Canaria, cochineal and wine. And when the other crops were blighted by plagues or foreign competition, the British introduced the cultivation of bananas and tomatoes.

Miller and Elder, whose warehouses still stand in the Parque Santa Catalina in Las Palmas, were largely responsible for opening up and developing the import-export trade which eventually prompted the Spanish government to nominate Las Palmas a Free Trade port. The water and electricity supplies were also set up by the British. Moreover, the second staple food of the Canary islanders (*gofio*, toasted cornflour, is the first) is the potato or *papa* which was grown from British seed – though an Englishman today would be hard-put to recognise the King Edward potato in the spud the Canaries call *papa kinewa*!

Cosmopolitan Community

Tourism, which represents a somewhat unbalanced 80 percent of the total income and employment of the island, has gradually brought people from all parts of the world to Gran Canaria – and a great many have stayed, attracted by the benign climate and, above all, the easy-going pace of life and the hospitality of the local community. There are Japanese, German, British and French schools on the island – and even a community of Korean nuns. Although the times when the people of Gran Canaria left their front doors open at night and invited complete strangers to share their meals are things of the past, the most lasting impression that visitors take away is of the extraordinary hospitality of this island.

Nevertheless, as in the times of their forefathers, the people of Gran Canaria reveal a united front when faced with people who have come here merely to make a quick killing from the tourist business. Such people are given the derogatory title of *godos* (Goths) by the islanders and it is not unusual to see rubbish bins sprayed with the words *Godos aquí* ('deposit Goths here').

Gran Canarians view the gradual process of integration into the EU with mixed feelings: on the one hand, they are enthusiastic about belonging to the European Union – perhaps more so than mainland Spaniards – but on the other fear the economic consequences for the islands, which some predict the Community will ignore. In any event, as has been the case in the past, the islanders are likely to adapt cheerfully to the new set of circumstances and strive to maintain the quality of the peaceful life they have long defended. Gran Canaria has the added status of the archipelago's capital – Las Palmas de Gran Canaria – although the administration is shared with Santa Cruz in Tenerife.

Although the pace of life is easy-going and the temperature is a balmy 22°C (71°F) average all year round, inviting visitors to lie back and relax, this does not mean that Gran Canaria is not moving with the times. The major facelift undergone by Las Palmas de Gran Canaria in the mid-1990s, the plans afoot for development as an off-shore trading zone, and large-scale building projects such as the new auditorium and convention centres show that Gran Canaria is moving determinedly into the 21st century.

Tourism produces 80 percent of island income

Historical Highlights

BC The Greeks and the Romans mention the Canary Islands in their texts. They refer to them as the *makaron nesoi*, the Gardens of the Hesperides, the Land of Eternal Spring and the Fortunate Islands. At that time, the islands were also probably known to the Phoenicians.

1st century AD Pliny writes of the expedition sent to the islands by King Juba II of Mauretania. The expedition brings back two enormous dogs. No mention is made of the islands being inhabited though it is thought that the natives, the Guanches, may have hidden in caves to avoid detection, as has been proved in the case of the island of Lanzarote.

1367 The Canaries appear on a map for the first time.

1475–83 The island is constantly under attack, first by the Portuguese and then by the Spaniards under different leaders but financed by the Catholic Monarchs, Ferdinand and Isabella.

The whole island of Gran Canaria submits to Pedro de Vera in 1483. This is largely due to the help of Tenesor Semidan, a *guanarteme* from the north who is captured, baptised a Christian under the name of Fernando Guanarteme and help to convince his fellow islanders to surrender. Many of the other *guanartemes*, the local chieftains, throw themselves off the clifftops rather than submit.

1478 The first city, the Real de Las Palmas, is founded on Gran Canaria by the Crown of Castile.

1492 Christopher Columbus stops off here on his first voyage to the New World. He repairs the rudder of *La Pinta* and the sail of *La Niña* (between the 25 August and the 1 September, according to the logbook). He returns to Las Palmas on his second and fourth voyages.

15th and 16th centuries The Portuguese set up sugar plantations and mills in the south. They bring slaves from Africa. Attacks from Sir Francis Drake and the Dutch under Van der Hoes are repelled.

1526 Royal Tribunal established in Gran Canaria for the settlement of local disputes.

18th and 19th centuries The main exports are wine and cochineal. The British set up a consulate on the islands from 1856 onwards. British settlers lay down the foundations of the import/export trade and play a large part in achieving water and electricity supplies. Coaling stations are set up in the harbour area to refuel transatlantic shipping.

1843 Benito Pérez Galdós, one of Spain's greatest novelists of all time, is born in Las Palmas de Gran Canaria.

1852 The islands are declared a Free Trade zone. The first tourists arrive on the islands.

1870s Gran Canaria still only has barely 10 miles of real road.

1927 The Canary Islands are divided into two provinces, East and West.

1936 Francisco Franco leaves Las Palmas for Spain and the Spanish Civil War begins.

1983 The Canary Islands are granted autonomous government but remain part of Spain.

1990 The island population reaches 600,000, with 355,000 living in the city of Las Palmas.

Las Palmas & The North

Gran Canaria is extraordinarily and naturally beautiful, but this beauty is not always instantly visible. The tourist may well feel distinctly un-seduced as the airport bus runs past barren landscapes dotted with cement plants and and necessary, but hardly picturesque, water purifying complexes towards Las Palmas de Gran Canaria; the road south of the airport to the resorts is no better, lined with skeletons of rudimentary plastic greenhouses. The grey colour of the houses is the result of a municipal tax: if you don't paint your house, you don't have to pay it.

But there is plenty to look forward to: as the bus rounds the corner after the dismal water-plant, Las Palmas de Gran Canaria stretches along the coast, basking like a lazy lizard in the sun. Down South, the bus rounds the bend to reveal miles of golden sands. This is what Gran Canaria is all about.

Gran Canaria's northern coast, with Las Palmas in the distance

1. City Sights

Around Vegueta and along the old shopping street of Triana to the Pueblo Canario. Evening on Las Palmas' beach promenade at Las Canteras. Wear comfortable shoes for the cobblestones. On Tuesday and Sunday there are folk dances and songs in the Pueblo Canario. The majority of the museums are closed on Monday. Shops reopen at 4.30pm on Triana.

–To starting point: number 1 bus from Parque Santa Catalina to the end of the line: Teatro Pérez Galdós. Journey takes about 20 minutes. See map on page 22.–

Las Palmas stretches along 9.5km (6 miles) of coast; this itinerary begins in the old part of town, and ends near the port in the commercial centre.

The **Teatro Pérez Galdós** is named after the famous Spanish realist novelist, Benito Pérez Galdós, born in Las Palmas. Alighting from your bus or taxi here, you are now at the crossroads between **Triana**, one of the main shopping areas, and **Vegueta**, the old quarter of the city and the original Real Las Palmas. Walk up past the theatre and cross over at the first pedestrian crossing. The road you are crossing used to be a fast-flowing river, which in times of heavy rainfall occasionally threatened to sweep away the Puente de Piedra (the bridge no longer exists but once stood by the next pedestrian crossing up), which joined Triana to Vegueta and allowed access to the Cathedral. On your left, on the corner of Mendizabal street, is the oldest of the local markets, probably worth a visit on the way back if you are interested in sampling local cheeses and produce.

Turn along the second street on your right to catch the atmosphere of Vegueta: Calle Pelota is chock-a-block with old haberdasheries, ironmongers, antique shops and pet shops (including feathered canaries). At the end of the street, you face the erstwhile Cine Avellaneda, now the **Teatro Guiniguada** and used to host literary events (writers Tom Sharpe and John Fowles have both spoken here) and art seminars. Turn left past some of the oldest buildings in Las Palmas up to the back of the Cathedral where you will find the **Casa de Colón** (the House-Museum of Columbus: Monday to Friday 9.30am–5.30pm, Saturday 10am–1pm), worth a visit to see what Canary-style houses are like at their best. Inside are interesting artefacts and weapons of the time of the discovery of the Americas, together with the maps of the voyages.

Casa de Colón

Coming out of the Casa de Colón, head along the street which borders the right side of the Cathedral (Calle Herrería) to come out onto the **Plaza Santa Ana**. This is the main square in Vegueta where

Las Palmas

you will find, at one end, the old **Town Hall** building and opposite, at the other end, the **Catedral Santa Ana**. It is almost *de rigueur* to have your photo taken beside the bronze dogs, the *canes* who gave their name to the Canary Islands. Sit beside them at the entrance to the square. One of the dogs was stolen not so many years ago by an enterprising thief; it was replaced but never recovered.

The Cathedral dominates the skyline in the old part of the city and, apart from being an obvious choice for photographers (especially when it is floodlit at night) it is well worth a visit. You have to enter by a door on the Calle Espíritu Santo, on the east side of the building. Since this is the entrance also to the **Museum of Religious Art** (Monday to Friday 9am–1.30pm and 4–6.30pm, Saturday 9am–2pm), you can visit both at the same time. This little museum, totally privately funded, houses a magnificent collection of Spanish colonial art. Unfortunately, its greatest treasures – leather-bound manuscripts and jewel-encrusted chalices and caskets – are not on public display because there are no glass cases in which to exhibit them and the two highly enthusiastic young guides find it difficult to be in all places at once. However, in a side chapel of the Cathedral, you can see the famous *Pendón de la Conquista* (The Banner of the Conquest) embroidered by the Catholic Monarch,

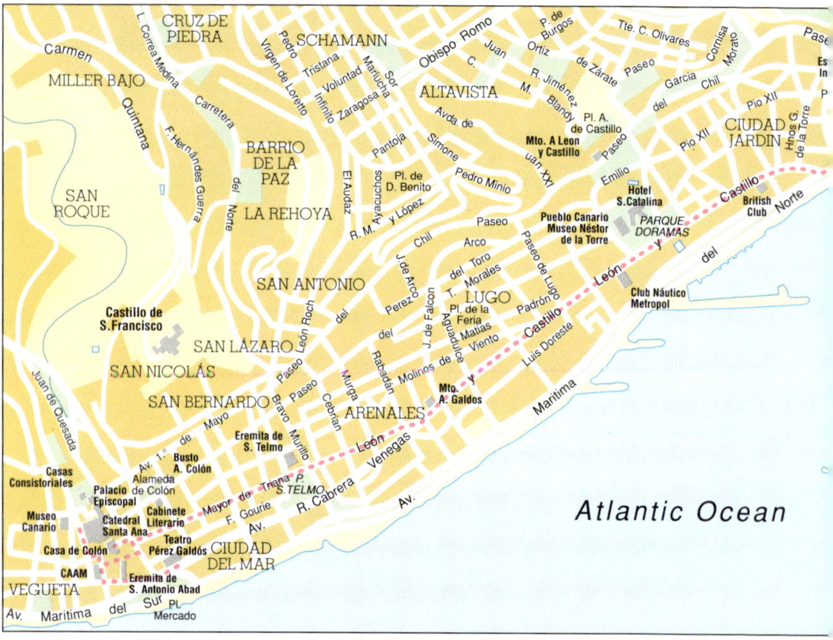

Canario and canary

Queen Isabella herself. This side chapel is shared by the seemingly immortal remains of Bishop Codina who, quite honestly, looks a little the worse for wear.

Come out onto Calle Espíritu Santo and turn left behind the Cathedral to admire the balconies and the fountain in the square. From the square, turn down to the right to the Calle de los Balcones which, apart from being one of the most typical and well-kept streets in Vegueta and an obvious target for photographers, houses the CAAM (the Atlantic Centre of Modern Art, Tuesday to Saturday 10am–9pm; Sunday 10am–2pm). This centre, in conjunction with other museums and art galleries on the international circuit, organises major exhibitions. Together with the Reina Sofía in Madrid and the IVAM in Valencia it ranks among the three main museums of modern art in Spain. The building itself is worth a visit to see how cleverly the traditional Canary architecture has been adapted to the needs of a modern art gallery.

On Plaza Santa Ana

Back up the cobbled pedestrian precinct of Calle de los Balcones and along to the right, past one of the oldest barber's shops in town and an interesting shop selling religious statues of all shapes and sizes, you wind through a short narrow alleyway (Calle Algaba) to come out onto the square of the shrine/chapel of **San Antonio Abad** where Christopher Columbus reputedly heard Mass before setting off on his voyage of discovery. Opposite is a local handicraft shop where you will find some of the best (and cheapest) sou-

venirs in town – cheap because they are nearly all produced by prisoners in the local jail.

By now, you may be in need of a little light refreshment. Should you want to try a vegetarian restaurant (remember that Gran Canaria produces wonderful tomatoes, avocados, cucumbers, courgettes etc), make your way to **Hippocrates** which is along a narrow street opposite San Antonio Abad. The restaurant is very close to the house where the famous Spanish tenor, Alfredo Kraus, was born (and still lives when he is in town). Should you require something more substantial, just a few yards along the road from the market, in the direction of the Calle de los Balcones, is **El Herreño** (Calle Mendizabal). Here you can sample the joys of *papas arrugadas con mojo* (small salty potatoes served with a hot paprika-based dip) as well as many other regional delicacies at very reasonable prices.

Pérez Galdós in stone

After lunch, cross back over to **Triana** where you started but this time via the Alameda de Colón where you can admire the magnificent building of the **Gabinete Literario**. Wind your way right down the Calle Malteses to Triana itself. Remember that the shops do not usually open until 4.30pm, so if you want to do more than window-shop take your time over lunch.

The pedestrian precinct here is full of interesting, good value shops, some of which have been established for many years. In particular, look out for **Metharam**, whose front is decorated with carved wooden elephants' heads, and for the antiques shop **Estoril** (next door) where real collectors' items are craftily hidden behind

San Antonio Abad

a barrage of cheap but colourful costume jewellery. **Maya**, at the end of the road, on the corner with the **Parque San Telmo**, is probably the best value shop in town for cameras, electrical goods, gadgets, etc.

At the far end of the Parque San Telmo, opposite the military headquarters from where Franco announced his military *coup* on the 18 July 1936, there is a delightful *art nouveau* kiosk which is worth a visit for a quiet drink. If you are feeling energetic, stroll along León y Castillo, passing the **Plaza de la Feria** where there is a fearful statue of Pérez Galdós framed against the background of the **Gobierno Civil** (watch out for the Civil Guards wearing their typical *tricornios*) and, opposite, the **Comandancia Marina**. You should bear in mind that the Comandancia Marina used to be on the seafront and that all the buildings along the **Avda Marítima** are built on land reclaimed from the sea. The harbour was formerly located at this end of the town, and there is still a red-light district here, though the 'ladies of leisure' are definitely in the veteran league.

Continue along León y Castillo for the **Pueblo Canario** (the Canary Village) which is some 20 minutes' walk from Triana. It is not a particularly scenic walk, so if you are feeling tired, jump into a taxi. The Pueblo Canario, in the grounds of the magnificent **Hotel Santa Catalina** (one of the oldest and most emblematic buildings in Las Palmas), was designed by the famous Canary painter Néstor de la Torre and built by his brother, Manuel Martín Fernández de la Torre. The **Museum of Néstor de la Torre** (Tuesday to Friday 10am–1pm and 4–8pm, Sunday 11am–1pm), in the Pueblo Canario is well worth a visit. Behind the **Bodegón** (another excellent place to eat) in the Pueblo, is a park which was formerly a mini-zoo with lions and bears but which now only sports two tired turtles. In front of the hotel is a statue commemorating the fall of the original local chieftains, the *guanartemes*, who, rather than submit to Spanish rule, committed suicide by throwing themselves off the cliffs.

Kiosk on Parque San Telmo

Enjoy a late afternoon cocktail of local rum (*Arehucas-Carta de Oro*) and coke on the verandah of the Hotel Santa Catalina and browse around

Dancer at the Pueblo Canario

the shops in the Pueblo Canario where, if nothing else, you can view a representative sample of everything which is typical of Gran Canaria (*timples*, a musical instrument like a tiny guitar; *naifes*, Canary knives; embroidered tablecloths and typical Canary costumes). Then you can either stroll a little further along to the **British Club**, where the expats congregate, near the end of León y Castillo, next door to what used to be the Hotel Metropole and is now the Town Hall, and then back along the seafront to the Parque Santa Catalina and a well-earned rest in the park itself (recently revamped).

Alternatively take a stroll along the **Paseo de las Canteras**, the beach-front promenade from where, if the day is clear, you will see the sun setting over Mount Teide in Tenerife. If the whole day has been too strenuous already, then take a taxi back to your hotel and unwind in your room; however, if you would like to cool off with a swim, head for the beach. An evening dip is part of the daily ritual in Las Palmas, and Las Canteras beach is one of the finest to be found in the whole of Spain, even though it is within the city itself.

After your swim, since the day has already been rather long and hard on the feet, stroll along the Paseo de las Canteras towards the Hotel Imperial Playa end (towards the east) where, next door to the hotel, you will find **Casa Carmelo**. This restaurant looks out over the sea and is excellent for meat (try their *solomillo* – sirloin) or fish (try the *sama* – sea bream or the *viejas* – parrotfish). As you are not driving anywhere this evening, indulge in a good wine; if you like white, try the local El Grifo from Lanzarote, a malmsey which comes in three versions with the medium-dry possibly the best.

Still feeling active? Then stroll back towards the Hotel Meliá where in the basement, you will find **El Coto**, a disco favoured by the older generation in Las Palmas (which here means everybody over 21). Or if you feel in the mood for something more romantic and mellow, the piano-bar on the first floor of the same hotel offers a spectacular view over the beach. Its Cuban pianist will play all your favourite tunes. Afterwards enjoy a nightcap of *cubalibre* (made with the wonderful Cuban Habana Club rum) and a stroll back along the beach to your hotel.

Las Canteras beach

2. To the Finger of God

Via Guía and Gáldar to Reptilandia and the Dedo de Dios (God's Finger). Return via the Valle de Agaete. With stops en route, this itinerary takes approximately 6 hours. The road is fairly straightforward with no great bends until you are in the Valle de Agaete. Remember that you will be changing altitude – Los Berrazales is 400m (1,312ft). Puerto de las Nieves is a pebble beach so take appropriate footwear.

–To starting point: Drive up Luis Morote, past Parque Santa Catalina and turn left at end along Bernardo de la Torre. Turn right at the first traffic lights and you are on Guanarteme.–

Your own transport is required for this itinerary. When choosing your vehicle, remember that a convertible, though great for the coast, is often unsuitable for drives into the interior, where changes in altitude and therefore temperature can be sudden.

Drive out of Las Palmas following the signposts for Agaete. At the end, you will see the road to the north (Norte) clearly signposted. Drive out along the C-810, past the spectacular Auditorium, stopping off briefly at **El Rincón**, to admire the view and the impressive volcanic rock sculpture, *Atlanta*, by the Canary artist Tony Gallardo. Be careful not to stray too close to the edge of the rocks here since the site is badly cared for and the fence has been knocked away in some places.

The road out through San Andrés and Bañaderos is hardly what you would call exciting although the view over the saltpans (Las Salinas) just outside **Bañaderos** is worth a stop and a photograph (where you see the sign 'Tiro Olímpico – 9km', pull off to the

right). Just before the spectacular soaring bridge of Puente de Silva is a turning off to the left which you reach via a roundabout; the road winds up to the **Cenobio de Valerón** (signposted) one of the few archaeological sites open to the public but ever more in danger of being closed. The steps up to this Guanche granary hewed out of the rock are extremely perilous and you will receive no help from the attendant, who is fairly old and taciturn.

Cenobio de Valerón

Looking out from this viewpoint, you can see the high rock from which it is alleged the last *guanarteme*, Bentejuí, threw himself. (See *History and Culture* section, page 12). The Puente de Silva is bedecked with wire netting to prevent contemporary Canary islanders from attempting to emulate him.

Back in your vehicle on the C-810, you will soon pass through a series of tunnels, after which you will notice banana plantations on both sides of the road, signifying that you are now passing though the island's main banana-growing area.

Local crop

You will now pass through the two rival towns of **Guía,** famous for its rennet cheese (*queso flor de Guía*) and **Gáldar**, the pre-Spanish capital of Gran Canaria. On the road between the two, on the left-hand side, shortly before entering Gáldar, stand the **Leacock** buildings, testimony to the beneficial influence of the British on Gran Canaria. Leacock was one of the British settlers who started up the banana export industry. On his death, he bequeathed his business to his workers (unfortunately it has since gone bankrupt).

Gáldar, like Guía before it, is not enormously impressive but you should visit the **Cueva Pintada** (well signposted but with little space for parking) which is decorated with the geometric drawings also found on the prehistoric Guanche *pintaderas* (terracotta and wooden seals which are believed to have been used either to tattoo the body or to identify the different families' stores of grain). The other archaeological site, lately restored, is the **Túmulo**

Cave house, Sardina del Norte

de la Guancha (a Guanche necropolis) which is reached via the scariest narrow road off the main plaza, bordered by high breeze-block walls. Just behind the site of the Túmulo is a natural rock-pool which is used by the locals as a swimming pool. Stop off for a quick dip.

Just beyond Gáldar, a road forks off to the west, towards **Sardina del Norte**. This small fishing village has a charming beach which is great for underwater swimming and snorkelling. If you take the road as far as it goes, you will come to a restaurant, perched on the rocks, where the fish and seafood are kept in wide open tanks full of constantly running water. If you are not too hungry at this point in the day, settle for a quick snack or *tapa* here then head back to the main road (C-810) and on to Agaete.

At the crossroads with Hoya de Pineda, you will see the signpost for **Reptilandia** (Monday to Sunday 11am–5.30pm), a reptile park run by a British couple and their Canary partner. Here you can see chameleons, lizards, giant tortoises and crocodiles in open enclosures resembling their natural habitat. The monkeys, tarantulas, poisonous toads, snakes, and the latest acquisition, the hissing cockroaches, are all either in cages or in glass cases. But you *can* enjoy the sensation of being embraced in the coils of Monty the python and find out that snakes are not at all slimy.

Reptilandia

Back on the C-810, the road winds down past the **Cuevas de las Cruces**, a system of caves on the left-hand side of the road (unfortunately they seem to have been used as makeshift loos for bus trips), past the inhabited cave houses on the right-hand side of the road and into **Agaete**. As you enter town, turn down to the right, behind the **church of La Concepción** (17th-century) where the signpost indicates **Puerto de las Nieves**. This is a small fishing village with a pebbly beach and one of the most characteristic views of

Gran Canaria: the rocky outcrop known as **El Dedo de Dios** (God's Finger). Park wherever you can in the square but try to avoid leaving your vehicle too close to the camels and donkeys, which provide rides for the young and the not so young.

There are several excellent restaurants in Puerto de las Nieves but perhaps the best is **El Dedo de Dios**, from which you can view the famous rock. Puerto de las Nieves is known for many things, among which are the hilarious blunders made in the translations of the menus in its restaurants (though with the introduction of Translation Studies in the University of Las Palmas things are gradually changing for the better in this regard). In any case, do not be worried by dishes such as 'rape sailor-style' since what they are really offering is *rape a la marinera* (a local fish served with a herby sauce garnish).

After lunch, take a stroll along the Paseo de los Poetas. Then, before going back to your car, pay a visit to the **Ermita de las Nieves**, which contains a magnificent 16th-century Flemish triptych that has recently been restored.

El Dedo de Dios (God's Finger)

Drive back to Agaete and take the road to the east signposted **El Valle**. The road gradually winds its way up through this incredibly beautiful valley, past **La Casa Romántica** (wonderful for coffee and cakes and soon to be the site of an 'adventure holiday' hotel) until you come to the hotel at **Los Berrazales**. Be warned: the bend just before the hotel, immediately after the water bottling factory, is a particularly dangerous one, especially if you meet the local bus coming the other way, so take care. There used to be a spa at Los Berrazales; this no longer exists but the exhilarating view down the valley is an experience in itself.

The neo-Gothic San Juan Bautista

Only the truly adventurous should continue up this road, which peters out at El Sao before the Pinar de Tamadaba (if you do venture this far you will be rewarded by heady views). Otherwise, take the same road back down, after some light refreshment, of course, and back to Las Palmas.

To introduce something new on the way back, take the road off to the right just before reaching Bañaderos, signposted **Arucas**. Then twist your way up the Montaña to be rewarded by another magnificent view over the neo-Gothic church of **San Juan Bautista** (sometimes wrongly referred to by the locals as 'the Cathedral' on account of its size) and over the bay of Las Palmas. There is a restaurant on the top of the hill, so you can sip a Tia Maria liqueur whilst enjoying the view. Then back to Las Palmas via the main road (C-810). On the way, you may want to stop off at Las Arenas, a big new shopping complex to see what the locals eat, at the best prices in town, in Continente – and if you are craving a Big Mac, this is the place to find one.

In the evening, treat yourself to something completely different. **El Hamburgo**, Calle Mari Sánchez (tel: 222745), as the name indicates, is a German restaurant. To find it, again stroll east along Las Canteras beach past the Hotel Imperial Playa and when the beachfront walk ends, turn up to the right, up Mari Sánchez (formerly called General Orgaz), where you will see the restaurant on the right-hand side of the road. The Canary owner Manolo and his German wife will give you a night to remember, with the best in German cuisine plus Manolo's entertaining repartee. He speaks at least five languages fluently and is mischievous in all of them. Be sure to save some space for the scrumptious desserts.

After dinner, stroll back down to the beachfront and, just before you get to the Hotel Imperial Playa, turn left down the Calle Ferrera where you will see **La Posada** on the right. Here, you will find all the combinations of coffee and liqueurs that you could possibly imagine. Relax over your favourite combination, then retire to your hotel.

Manolo in El Hamburgo

3. To the Top of the Island

This six-hour itinerary goes via the Jardín Canario up to the Pinar de Tamadaba (which lies 1,444m/4,737ft above sea level so take some warm clothing in case you get cold). It offers spectacular views all the way along a route that takes in La Atalaya, San Mateo and Artenara. The local fiestas 'del Almendro en flor' – to celebrate the flowering of the almond trees – are usually held at the end of January.

–To starting point: Drive along the Avda. Marítima and turn off to the left at the flyover/Pérez Galdós theatre. From there take the c-811 to Tafira. *See map on page 28.–*

The road up to Tafira is commonly referred to as the 'Scalextric route' by locals, on account of its many terrible bends and the speed of the traffic. (In particular, you are advised to look out for two bends just beyond the Tropical beer factory.) Drive straight up the Llano de las Brujas where, if you look down to the right, you will see the old folks' home. Now move into the right-hand lane, even at the risk of getting caught behind one of the UTINSA buses (slow-moving and belching disgusting exhaust fumes), past the University campus in Tafira Baja and look out for the sign for the **Jardín Canario**, the first stop.

Park outside the restaurant and enter the gardens by the top gate. Gradually work your way down through the grounds admiring the magnificent collection of local flora on show including the legendary *dragos*, the dragon-trees, and the cactus garden.

Unfortunately, the hike back to the car is no stroll but you can reward yourselves at the top with a cooling local beer (Tropical, of course) and goat's cheese (*queso tierno*) at El Jardín Canario. There are magnificent, far-reaching views to be enjoyed from the closed balcony.

Suitably refreshed, climb back into the car. Take care leaving the gardens since cars whizz along this part of the road at great speed and you will also have to move over into the fast lane as quickly as possible. Continue up through the narrow part of Tafira, past one of the first hotels to be built on the island, Los Frailes, on your left, and follow the signs to the golf course of Bandama, which is perched on top of the volcanic crater of the same name. The **Caldera de Bandama**, at 574m (1,889ft) offers spectacular views over Las Palmas. If you look hard, you will notice a house nestled at

Beware of pedestrians on the Tafira road

Earthenware

the foot of the crater. The old man who lives there climbs up and down the crater every day and, logically enough, has no problems either with robbers or with his animals escaping.

The **Golf Club of Bandama** was founded by the British community, which still tends to centre around Tafira, possibly because the climate here is cooler and wetter than elsewhere on the island and therefore more reminiscent of home. This is the oldest golf club in Spain (set up in 1891) and its nine holes are very carefully tended. Golf is now an up-and-coming sport in Spain, with the Ballesteros and Olazábals of the world blazing trails of glory. The Caldera is also a favourite haunt of local courting couples (also, perhaps, because it is cooler); watch out for oddly parked cars.

A road runs along the side of the golf course, past the British School and the riding school to the cave village of **La Atalaya**, famous for its earthenware pottery, which is hand-moulded and left to bake in the sun. The most famous of the potters, Panchito, died a few years ago but his disciples make sure that his memory lives on in their splendid artworks. To enter the village turn right at the crossroads and then up to the left; the best views and best pottery are to be found down a flight of steps behind the village square where the church stands.

Roads here are narrow and twisting

Once back in the car, and if you are feeling adventurous, follow the narrow road up behind the church. A very rudimentary traffic-light, which works highly efficiently nonetheless, controls the traffic up to **La Concepción**, one of the most exclusive residential sites on the island thanks to its magnificent views. The little shrine on the left, now almost abandoned to its fate, is the oldest *ermita* on the island.

Back down the slope and turn down to the left beside the church square. Another turn left will take you down the Carretera de la Atalaya to the main road. Turn left at the crossroads but be careful because visibility to the right is very poor. You will now pass through **Santa Brígida** where Dutch invaders, under Van der Hoes, were driven back and out of Gran Canaria by the islanders in 1599. Continue on the C-811, running past Pino Santo on the right and the old British country club, now turned into a restaurant called Monte Verde, on your left.

A little farther up the road, also on the left, in El Madroñal, you will see the restaurant **Martel** (open every day). The owner of this typical Canary restaurant also has one of the best wine-cellars on the island and offers a wide variety of cheeses and olives in *mojo* (a delicious herb sauce).

Roadside shrine

Back in the car, continue up the road to **San Mateo** where, shortly after an incongruously ugly statue presumably representing the noble peasant, on the right, you will see the ethnological museum of **Cho Zacarías** (Monday to Saturday 9.30am–1pm; closed Sunday and local holidays; entrance fee). This is well worth an unhurried visit; if there are coaches parked outside, it is best to take a stroll round the village first, calling in at the **Pastelería San Mateo**, just a little farther up the pavement, where you will be able to buy the delicious *bienmesabe*, a sticky honey and almond confection. The local market, also worth a look inside, is along the first road on your left.

You best option for lunch is the restaurant in Cho Zacarías (closed Monday), but make sure you give yourself plenty of time to look round the museum first. The restaurant is also decorated with exhibits, including typical farming implements and an enormous bellows beside the fireplace. The food is always delicious and the owner, who speaks both English and German, will be pleased to recommend dishes.

After lunch, prepare for the winding, hair-raising drive up through the mountains (there is a particularly nasty bend at La Lechuza) to **Cruz de Tejeda** at 1,450m (4,757ft) following the signposts. The cross, one of many different types to be seen at high-standing locations, is intended to mark the supremacy of Christianity. The **Parador**, a castle-like construction, is worth a visit, not least to take photos of **Roque Nublo, Roque Bentaiga** and **El Fraile**, three spectacular volcanic rock outcrops, from the terrace. You may want to have a drink and a rest here – you have changed altitude very abruptly and may be feeling it.

If you are not already exhausted, return to the C-811, and drive back to a fork signposted for **Artenara** (see *Itinerary 4*). The road to Artenara winds around gorges and terraced landscapes but affords wonderful views. The village itself is tiny. Just before the village square, down to the right, look for a signpost for **La Silla**. This restaurant is entered via a tunnel, at the end of which you will be welcomed by the most spectacular view, weather permitting, of Roque Nublo and the Bentaiga. This restaurant is well worth visiting on its own (anyone who has not stayed the pace should not despair since it is included in another itinerary in this book). For those who want to experience life as a cave-dweller, several caves have been converted into accommodation as part of a programme for rural tourism.

Back in the car, continue along the same road, which gradually winds its way up to the dizzy heights of the **Pinar de Tamadaba,** 1,444m (4,737ft). This spectacular pine forest offers fabulous views over Agaete and even as far as Mount Teide on Tenerife, if the weather is clear.

Photographers should make their way back to Las Palmas via **Valleseco** (well signposted). In Valleseco itself, if you have not already taken enough breathtaking pictures, the restaurant on the right-hand side of the road, **El Balcón de Zamora**, offers you the possibility for a few more.

The next stop on this winding road is the village of **Teror** (GC-230 again, well signposted). Teror is good for a leisurely stroll, not least for its splendid wooden balconies and typical Canary architecture. The recently reopened **Casa-Museo de los Manrique** is also well worth a visit to see how the island's upper echelons used to live (open 11am–7.30pm).

Also worth seeing in Teror is the **Basilica de Nuestra Sra del Pino**, the baroque-neoclassical temple which houses the **Virgen del Pino**, patroness of the island. A door behind the altar will allow you to get a closer glimpse of the statue of the Madonna, decked out in precious jewellery presented to the church by devotees who have

Typical balcony in Teror

View of Bentaiga

had their prayers answered by the Madonna (this jewellery has been stolen on more than one occasion). On 8 September each year (see *Calendar of Special Events, page 73*) people from all over the islands set off in groups to walk, or even crawl on their knees, along the road to the shrine.

Opposite the basilica, stallholders peddle an assortment of wares in the main square (a more elaborate street market is held on Sunday here) and a rather downtrodden-looking bar offers the chance to taste *chorizo de Teror* (the highly spiced local sausage whose memory lingers on your breath for quite a while afterwards) and, for those with a sweet tooth, *turrón* (a soft nougat made from *gofio*). If you are feeling particularly brave, you could also try the local rum as the natives drink it – on its own – but remember those twisting roads back to Las Palmas.

The road from Teror back to Las Palmas is, in fact, fairly fast at first; but after **Tenoya** it becomes narrow and winding. It then passes through Tamaraceite and back into **Las Palmas** via the Feria del Atlántico. If you look up to the left, at the second traffic lights, you will see the Feria: the Trade Fair precinct. (The Trade Fair takes place in April every year.) From here, continue straight down the hill, keeping in the left-hand lane, round the back of the football stadium and straight down to the Plaza de España. Here, turn second right off the roundabout and down Mesa y López, past the department stores Galerías Preciados. Follow this street as far as it goes and, at the end, turn left for the Parque Santa Catalina and familiar surroundings.

Teror's Virgen del Pino

Reward yourself at the end of this long day with a relaxing drink on the terrace of the **Hotel Meliá** on the Paseo de las Canteras (bearing east), followed by dinner in the beautifully decorated restaurant **El Jardín Botanico** in the same hotel, with its magnificent views over the beach. If you are not too tired after dinner, make for **Pachá**, a disco (Calle Simón Bolívar) along from the Elder and Miller buildings on Parque Santa Catalina, where you can bop the night away.

Alternatively, you may want just to enjoy the balmy night with a last drink on a terrace bar in the Parque itself.

4. Fontanales and Artenara

A morning excursion into the interior via Moya, incorporating the museum of an island poet, pine and laurel forests and a holy shrine. Especially recommended for those who missed out Artenara on Itinerary 3. A jeep is essential for the stretch which takes you through the Tilos de Moya to Fontanales.

–To starting point: leave Las Palmas via Guanarteme.
See map on p. 28.–

Follow the signposts out of Las Palmas in the direction of Agaete. The road runs along the coast but is marred by haphazard building work (islanders leave their properties unpainted in order to avoid the hefty taxes levied on finished buildings). Run through **Bañaderos** and take the turning off to the right, signposted **Pagador**. Follow the road round the bend, past a church with a painted representation of a stained-glass window and take the road signposted for **Moya**, which passes through **Cabo Verde**, steep in parts and extremely narrow in others but affording fine views.

The road enters Moya from below the square, where a fine church hangs perilously over the cliff-face (from here it is possible to take a great photograph right down the gully to the sea). Across from the square stands the **House-Museum of Tomás Morales**, one of the most famous poets of the Canary Islands (daily from 10am–2pm, closed holidays).

Follow the road round the bottom of the church and up to the right. This street takes you past the ladies selling *suspiros* (meringues) and *bizcochos* (sponge fingers), typical of Moya but not recommended if you are running a healthy thirst, and down to a crossroads. If you want an easy run up to Fontanales, turn up to the left, where the town is signposted.

Otherwise, and only if you are driving a jeep because the going is tough, continue straight on and take the next turning off to the left where **Los Tilos de Moya** is signposted. Much of this laurel forest has been closed to the public in an effort to halt environmental damage. The road (always open) is not often used and you can tell why; proceed slowly as it is narrow as well as winding and cars may come down in the opposite direction, often on a steep incline. However, the countryside is beautiful and the sense of travelling through parts of the island that even the natives do not know is exhilarating.

Fontanales is a typical Canary village nestling in a valley between vol-

Moya

Moya street

canic hills. If you have come via Los Tilos, you turn left at the main road and enter Fontanales the back way, past the church. Otherwise, you come in on the main road. Park near the **Restaurante Sibora** or the **Bar Fontanales**, good places in which to adjourn for a drink and a *tapa* (animal lovers are warned: the walls of the Bar Fontanales are adorned with the proud owner's hunting trophies).

Back on the road, on the right-hand side about 1km (½ mile) further on, is **El Cortijo**, one of the latest ventures in the development of rural tourism on Gran Canaria. As well as offering comfortable accommodation, it offers a range of local delicacies and wines, though on this itinerary I recommend you stop for lunch a little further on.

Regaining the main road, follow signposts to **Artenara**. Here, stop off to have lunch in the **Mesón de la Silla**, which besides serving good and reasonably-priced food in pleasant surroundings offers anyone who didn't follow Itinerary 3 the opportunity to photograph the peaks of **Roque Nublo** and **Roque Bentaiga** from the verandah. Artenara itself is not much more than a square but a little road running beside the church (best travelled on foot) will take you to the quaint grotto of the **Virgen de la Cuevita**, the site of an annual procession during August (see *Calendar of Special Events, page 73*).

Suitably refreshed, you can either drive back to Las Palmas, taking the route via **San Mateo** and **Santa Brígida** (the C-811) which you may have taken on Itinerary *3*, or, if you have time to spare (roughly one hour there and back) and did not choose the alternative route in Itinerary 3, continue on to the **Pinar de Tamadaba** (1½km/1 mile), the incredible pine forest which towers above Agaete and affords fine views of Mount Teide on Tenerife, provided the day is clear.

Whether or not you choose to go to the Pinar, you could return via **Hoya de Pineda** (slightly farther along the road from Artenara in the direction of Tamadaba), **Montaña Vergara**, back down past the Cenobio de Valerón (see *Itinerary 1*) and on to the main road back to Las Palmas via Bañaderos. This option is hair-raising at times but the magnificent views more than make up for that.

5. Barranco de Guayadeque

A half-day excursion to the deep ravine (Barranco) of Guayadeque via the windswept regions of Telde and Ingenio. Lunch in a cave restaurant in the Barranco where, on Sunday, holidays and other busy times, you can sample 'sancocho', a special fish dish.

–To starting point: Drive down Calle Nicolás Estevanez, past Parque Santa Catalina. Cross over Leon y Castillo at the traffic lights and turn third right to connect with the motorway down to the South (GC-1). Jeep advisable. *See map on page 42.**–*

Caves at Cuarto Puertas

Leave **Las Palmas** by the road for the airport and turn off where you see Telde signposted. **Telde**, *la ciudad de los muebles* (the city of furniture), has more furniture shops per square metre than any other town on the islands. Telde is also famous for its faith-healers, its superstitions and the fact that its inhabitants have won the Christmas national lottery prize (known as *El Gordo* or the fatty) more often than anywhere else in Spain including Madrid and Barcelona. Together with Gáldar, Telde was the main centre for the original Guanches and the site of the discovery of the emblematic *ídolo de Tara*, one of their cherished idols.

If you can find a parking space, the church of **San Juan** merits a visit, especially on account of its strange crucifix made out of corn cobs mounted on silver (Luján Pérez). The district of **San Francisco**, across the road, is also worth a stroll since here you

Looking down the Barranco

can see the most representative collection of Canary-style houses on the island. Back in the car, take the road for **Los Llanos** (C-812) to visit **Cuatro Puertas** site of one of the original *harimaguadas* (see *History and Culture, page 12*).

Continue down the C-812 past **Aguatona** towards Ingenio, named after the Portuguese for sugar-mill. This region was famous for its sugar-cane production, although it is much diminished nowadays. Just outside Ingenio, you should not miss **El Museo de Piedras** (daily 9am–6pm) which has a fascinating display of old farm tools and, as the name suggests, rocks. It also boasts a representative display of local handicrafts.

Back in the car, continue into Ingenio. At the crossroads, on the corner, you may see the locals selling *morenas*, big electric eels which are considered a great delicacy. It is worth turning right, where the **Barranco de Guayadeque** is signposted, then right again and into the town square. **Ingenio** was a town largely founded by the Portuguese and has inherited a tradition of witchcraft and superstition from the large slave population which inhabited it for a long time.

The road to the Barranco twists its way up then plunges suddenly downwards. The Barranco is most representative of what the Guanches' territory used to be like. The cliffs are dotted with caves hacked out of the walls, some for human habitation, others for housing goats.

Continue along the road to the right, winding up to the restaurant, itself housed in a maze of caves, which offers you, again, a breathtaking

Lacemaker in El Museo de Piedras

view down the gully. Here you can get typical Canary food. On Sunday and holidays the restaurant serves *sancocho* (salted fish served with boiled sweet potatoes and *mojo* and accompanied by *gofio* kneaded with milk and bananas – the speciality of the region); it is the only restaurant still to serve it. If you decide try it, make sure you drink plenty of water or beer because it will induce a thirst.

From the Barranco, wend your way down to **Agüimes**, whose carnival celebrations are said to beat any on the islands, down through **Vecindario** (formerly tomato-producing country) which is called *la ciudad de los Mercedes* on account of the many rich people who live there. Regain the main road back to Las Palmas, leaving behind the beaches of **Melenara**, **Playa del Hombre** and **La Garita**, small, badly maintained beaches which do not merit a stop-off unless you are desperately hot and dusty.

6. Las Palmas: Museums and Galleries

Most tourists to Gran Canaria are unaware of the wide range of art galleries and museums which are open to them and, with the weather so good, few people bother to find out. But if you want to take an afternoon off from sun-bathing there is plenty to see in the stimulating collections in Las Palmas de Gran Canaria. I suggest that you hop between these by taxi or bus (Lines 1 and 2 take you to Vegueta from the Parque Santa Catalina) since parking is a problem.

The most interesting small museum, without a shadow of a doubt, is the **Museo Canario**, Calle Dr Chil, Vegueta (Monday to Friday 10am–1pm and 4–7.30pm, Saturday 10am–1pm, Sunday 10am–2pm). It rates at least an hour's visit. Here you have one of the best collections of mummies in the world (recognised as such in the last unlikely-sounding International Mummy Congress, held in Puerto de la Cruz, Tenerife, in 1991). You can also see the vestiges of the pre-Conquest culture of the Guanches – their *pintaderas* (see *History and Culture, page 13*); their idols (*el ídolo de Tara*), reminiscent of monuments associated with fertility rites in Cornwall, England – and find out about the islands' customs. For

Home to a fine museum

Guanche mummy remains in the Museo Canario

example, did you know that the most common remedy for illness among the Guanches was *trepanación*, boring a hole in the head of the patient? Or that they could not swim? Or that the female sexual apparatus was so revered that it was painted over the walls of caves? The British novelist John Fowles, on a visit to Gran Canaria in 1991, described the museum as 'one of the finest small museums I have ever had the fortune to visit.' The Museo Canario also boasts an impressive library containing the original writings of the Marquis of Bute, one of the first tourists to visit the Canary Islands.

A little farther up the Calle Dr Chil, on the right-hand side, is the **Square of Santo Domingo**, another significant spot in Vegueta. It was here that the Guanches formally submitted to the Spanish invaders in the presence of the famous Banner of the Conquest (see *Itinerary 1*). Walk back down the far side of the church on the square, across Plaza Santa Ana and past the restoration work that is underway on the Episcopal Palace across from the Cathedral. Cross at the traffic lights.

On the far corner, opposite the Alameda de Colón (once an avenue lined with trees) you will find the CICA, the art gallery cum museum/conference centre run by the Caja de Ahorros (Savings Bank), another good venue for exhibitions. Retrace your steps and cross over to the other pavement at the traffic lights for the so-called **Plaza de las Ranas** (the Square of the Frogs – you should see why). You are probably able to resist the aromas of roast chicken and garlic potatoes at this time of day, but the Baskin-Robbins ice-cream shop may be too much of a temptation.

Ice-cream in hand, stroll down to the left past the recently re-opened **Biblioteca Insular** (Monday to Friday 10am–1pm and 4–8pm). This library is one of the best examples of late 19th-century architecture in Las Palmas.

Afterwards, make your way down the Calle Peregrina – look out for the artisan carpenter's next to the old printer's – and out onto

The Pérez Galdós Museum

the Calle Malteses. If you turn up to the left here, you will find an interesting haberdashery/lingerie shop selling all kinds of unusual underwear. Otherwise, turn down to the right and take the first left for the Calle Cano and the **Casa-Museo Benito Pérez Galdós** (Monday to Friday 9am–1pm and 4–8pm). Revered as one of the greatest Spanish novelists of all time and the ultimate exponent of realism in Spanish literature, Pérez Galdós was born and lived in this somewhat unpretentious house from 1843 to 1862. Among his work, his novels *Fortunata* and *Jacinta* are published in English by Penguin Classics.

Stroll along Calle Cano until it meets Viera y Clavijo. Along the way, observe the variety of architectural styles in this district, in particular the splendid examples of art nouveau and modernism. Look out for **Sayme** and **Madelca**, both of which sell prints of modern Canary artists. In Viera y Clavijo, you will find the tempting cake-shop and delicatessen **Morales**. If you are in the mood for something savoury, try a *sandwich de berros* (a watercress sandwich). There are so many delicious sweets to choose from, it is difficult to recommend any in particular but I suggest you try the San Marcos for size.

Stroll up Bravo Murillo to see the classic modernist building of the **Cabildo,** beside which is the **Centro Insular de Cultura** (Mon-

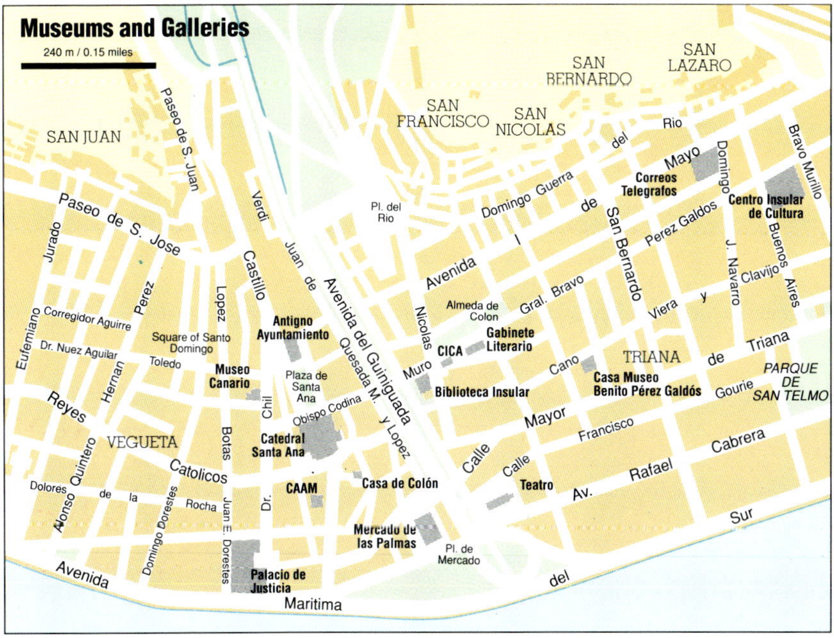

You might be lucky!

day to Friday 9am–2pm and 5–8pm), where you are sure to find an exhibition of traditional crafts, photography, art or architecture.

Now cross at the traffic-lights to catch a bus on the corner, past the bookshop **Librería Nogal**, where you can pick up books on the Canary Islands as well as English paperbacks.

If you prefer to take a taxi rather than a bus, hail one on the other side of the road. Cross back for the bus and buy a lottery ticket, the *ciegos* (so-called because it is run by ONCE, the Spanish Organisation for the Blind, one of the richest and most influential charities in the world). You never know – you might strike lucky.

From the Parque Santa Catalina, walk back to **La Regenta** (Calle León y Castillo, 427; Monday to Friday 11am–1pm and 6–9pm) which stages a range of excellent exhibitions by Canary artists and photographers.

7. Shopping in Las Palmas

Breakfast on Parque Santa Catalina followed by best buys – from silk blouses to electric gadgets – in Las Canteras.

Las Palmas is a duty-free port, so you can find goods from all parts of the world here and at bargain prices. There are three main shopping areas. The first, where I suggest you spend the morning, lies in the part of Las Palmas behind Parque Santa Catalina (between the port and the beach) which is commonly referred to as **Las Canteras**. The second is **Triana** where the Canary islanders shop and where the most 'typical' souvenirs related to Canary culture can be bought (see *Itinerary 1*). The third is the area around **Mesa y López**, halfway between Triana and Las Canteras and dominated by the two big department stores, **El Corte Inglés** and **Galerías Preciados**. This is the best place to shop for clothes.

Las Canteras offers something for everybody, including friends back home. Start off with a fortifying breakfast on one of the terraces on the **Parque Santa Catalina**. Ask for *chocolate con churros,* pastries that are dunked into thick hot chocolate – a typically Spanish start to the day.

Street sales

After breakfast, set off up the **Calle Ripoche**, off the middle of the square. This is 'haggling' territory where you can pick up real bargains if you know how to strike a mean deal. Most of these shops are owned by Hindus who, although born and brought up in Las Palmas, have not lost their traditions or habits, which include the superstition that should their first customer walk out empty-handed things will not go well all day. Many of them bless their establishment by sprinkling the entrance with holy water from the Ganges, witness **Perry's** in the Calle Luis Morote. On the third corner on the left in Ripoche is **Bazar Mavi,** excellent value for silk blouses and intricately crocheted tops. The tablecloths are also extremely good value. **Visanta**, a little further up on the left past the Levis shops, is one of the cheapest places for good quality cameras, watches, Ray-Ban sunglasses and electronic gear. Bargain hard.

Come out of Visanta and walk back down Ripoche in the direction of the Parque. This area of rundown shops and boarding houses is a favourite haunt of soldiers and sailors on leave from military service. Turn second left along **Secretario Artiles**, now occupied by stalls which were once on and around the Parque (it is advisable to keep out of shady side alleys). Down on your left is the novelty shop **Carrousel**, where you can buy a solar-powered toothbrush, china-soled socks which claim to stimulate the circulation, or tablets which when added to water turn into a complete set of cotton undies and a towel.

At the end of Secretario Artiles turn left into **Luis Morote**. Visit the **Perfumería Caribe** for a variety of duty-free perfumes – much cheaper than on the plane. This isn't the place for haggling but you may get little extras thrown in by appearing to be dubious! Although you are unlikely to be feeling the cold, why not prepare for harder times? Gran Canaria is one of the best places to buy leatherwear and fur coats, all of excellent quality and at superb prices. There is little demand among islanders – though on opening nights of opera, you will see a great many furs around the Teatro Pérez Galdós – so most trade comes from holidaymakers. **Peletería Helena** (Luis Morote) offers high quality clothes, with coats and jackets made to measure. A little further up Luis Morote, still on the left, **M Nanwani** specialises in

Shoppers in Triana

arts and crafts from all parts of the world. For great gifts, try **Marfil Dani** on the other side of Luis Morote opposite **Zorba's** the disco. Lucky pyramids, children's watches, even football fans (of the ventilating type) are all found here. For more trinkets, drop in to **Napoleon**, not surprisingly beside the Hotel Concorde on Tomás Miller (first on your right off Luis Morote).

Although not typical of the Canary Islands, **Lladró** porcelain is much sought after and heavily taxed on the mainland. The shop which offers the best selection of Lladró is **Nara**, also good value for spirits and tobacco, on the corner of Tomás Miller and the beach. Opposite the shop, on the beachfront, is a great beach shop, **Praia do Rio**, which has the best in Brazilian beachwear at cheap prices. Next door (Alfredo L Jones, 42), **Dracena** the florist can prepare an arrangement of strelitzias and anthurums for you to take back home. Flowers are very good value in Gran Canaria so make the most of them. Further down Alfredo Jones (pronounced 'hoanies' by the locals), on the right hand side is **Electronica Bel**, purveyor of luxury sheets – even silk ones if you feel so inclined – Habana Club rum (not available everywhere) and good cigars. Still hankering after a tablecloth? Cross over to **Artesanía Paquita** where you can buy the real thing, which is Canary drawn-thread embroidery work, highly expensive, or a much cheaper Chinese replica. Again, try to bargain.

Lastly, hop in to either **Lurueña** or **Lopez** (one on each corner) for classic footwear and the latest fashions respectively.

If after all that shopping you only want a light lunch, try **La Cafetera** (back up Alfredo Jones, opposite the Reina Isabel Hotel); its crêpes and cakes are so delicious that you may end up eating more than you planned. Good value for money is **La Strada**, up Tomás Miller on the left-hand side (cross back over Luis Morote). It offers an excellent self-service buffet where you can eat as much as you like for relatively few pesetas.

Elegant shopping, traditional-style

The South

Sun, Sea and Sand

The south of Gran Canaria is known for its beaches, and tourist development is extensive. Nonetheless there are many villages and coves (for example Tasarte, Tasartico and Veneguera) untouched by tourism. As a rule, native Gran Canarians tend to prefer the beaches of San Agustín, Las Meloneras and Montaña Arena.

8. Southern Beaches

Once you've become familiar with your own stretch of coastline, I suggest you try this full day sampling the idyllic coves of the coast west of Playa del Inglés, adjourning for a fish lunch en route. Take water or refreshment with you since most of these small beaches have no facilities.

–To starting point: Make your way to the GC-1.–

Follow the GC-1 until **Pasito Blanco**, a private marina which doesn't object to visitors during weekdays. On the hillside to the right, above the new campsite at Pasito Blanco, is the **Space Station**. Two bends on from here, take a dirt road off to the left (recognisable only by a dustbin which is there to collect rubbish from the ecologically-minded people who frequent this beach), which meanders down to a ramshackle hut surrounded by hen-coops and two or three stray dogs. Leave your car here; it will be quite safe. Now walk round the path to the left, over the rocks (easily followed), to **Montaña Arena**, a little-known beach frequented mainly by locals. A few

The South of Gran Canaria is a world apart. It caters for tourists who come in search of sun, sea, sand and organised entertainment, which is here aplenty. Remains of Guanches were found here during excavations for the new motorway, but they have been whisked out of public sight until the powers-that-be decide their fate. In the South, no-one in the tourist industry is interested in the past culture of the *Canarios*, not even the local press. Itineraries 8 and 9 can both be followed from southern resorts and will take you away from the crowded areas; the remaining itineraries highlight some of the best of the South's varied entertainments.

ships ferrying contraband have run aground here but, providing you watch out for where the sand shelves away abruptly, the beach is safe.

Back in the car after your swim, continue down the coast to **Arguineguin**. Avert your eyes when you come to the unlovely cement factory, but stop off at the new complex which has recently been built

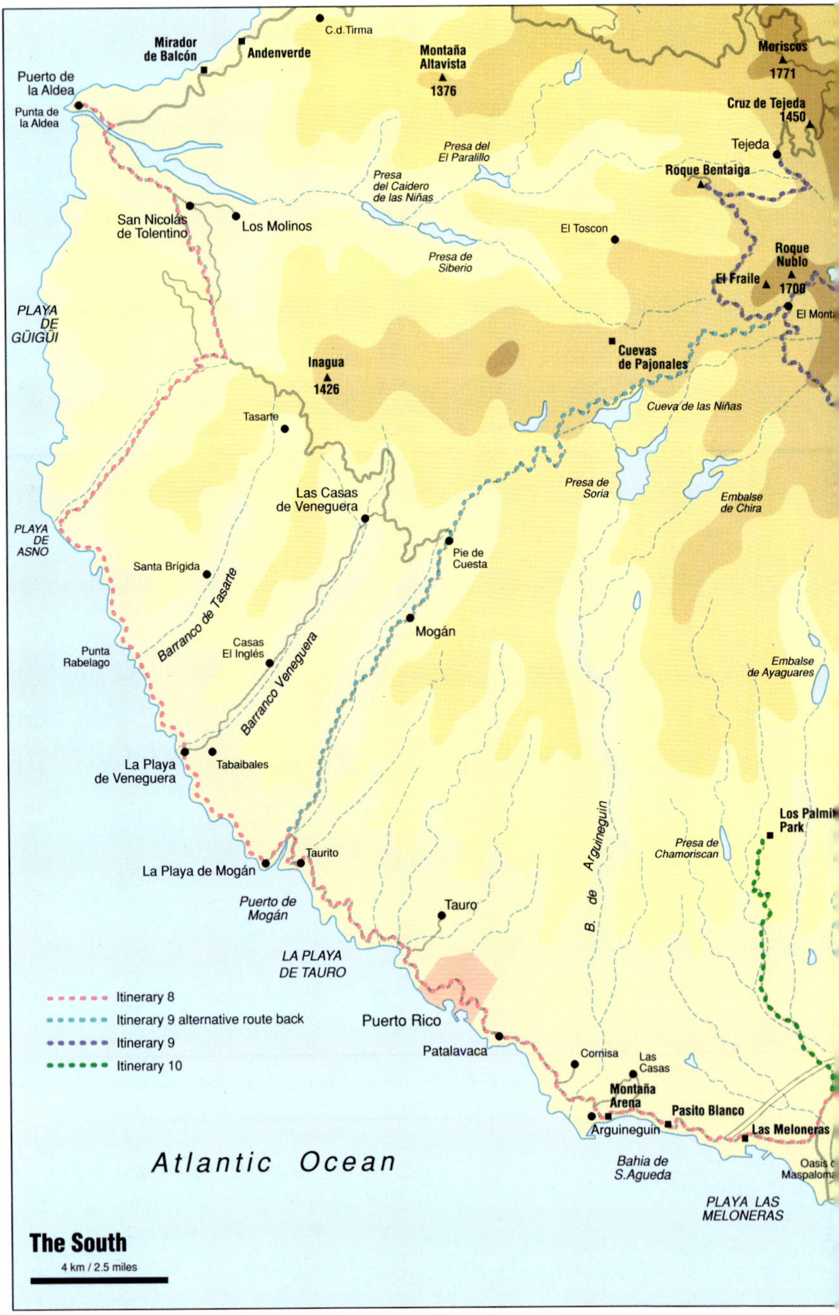

here and have a drink on one of the poolside verandahs. If you are hungry by now, you may want to try the restaurant **Hogar del Pescador**, a favourite haunt of international models and photo crews who come to the south of the island for fashion shoots. Though not obviously that promising (it is very rustic and just around the corner from the cement factory), its food is delicious, very fresh and ridiculously inexpensive.

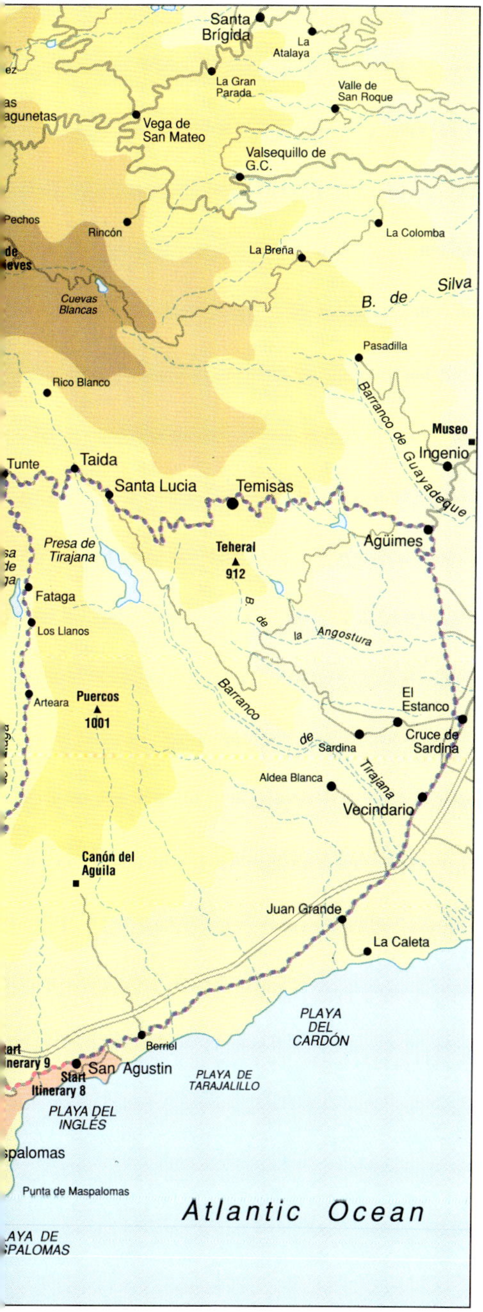

If you can survive a bit longer without sustenance, drive through **Patalavaca** and past the multiple hotels whose rooms hang perilously over the sea. One of them, **Aquamarina**, is beautifully landscaped and its restaurant, Aquarela, is ideal for a romantic (but not cheap) night out. Right next door is the new and popular time-share resort of Anfidel Mar. A little further on is **Los Caideros**, an enormous tourist complex built around a small and uninspiring beach, and beyond that **Puerto Rico**, which is tourism run amok. The best that can be said of Puerto Rico is that its beach is 'comfortable' for families with small children since it is too small for them to get lost. There are also plenty of facilites for water-skiing, sailing, wind-surfing and hiring paddle boats.

Continue along the road and, if you feel you could do with another swim, stop off at the **Barranco de Tiri-**

Bathing belle, Puerto Rico

taña (Lovers' Gulley), but be warned: the walk down to the sea is not leisurely.

Shortly before you come to Puerto de Mogán you will hit **Taurito**. The gigantic tourist complex that has been built around this small beach was so determined to make good use of the little space at its disposal that some of the hotel corridors are almost square up against the main road. The complex is unique on Gran Canaria, with a series of swimming pools in the style of Lago Martiánez in Puerto de la Cruz, Tenerife.

Further along, beyond a series of acute hairpin bends, is **Mogán**. The beach here is not impressive but the Venetian-style harbour area is very picturesque. Eat at the restaurant **Orilla del Mar** (no longer 'on the banks of the sea' as the name suggests), where fish is fresh and the salads are the best on the island (most of the avocados and papaws or papaya come from around here). Try papaw in Cointreau as a dessert – the fruit is reputed to have kept ex-President Reagan lively and is said to be a good digestive. The waiter, who is also the owner, may even give you a song if the restaurant is not too busy.

Suitably refreshed, continue along the coast, taking in the unspoilt beach of **Veneguera**, further along the road on the left. Pass by **Tasarte** and **Tasartico** (also good options for holidaymakers who like to get away from the crowded beaches of the resorts), up to **San Nicolás de Tolentino**, where you can visit the mini-zoo to see the eagle. On 10 September, San Nicolás de Tolentino celebrates the annual Fiesta del Charco (also see *Calendar of Special Events, page 73*). From here, drive onto **La Aldea** on the headland, which has proved a rich source of archaeological finds.

Again, there are two alternative routes here. You can either clamber over the rocks to the beach of La Aldea (only when the tide is not high) or, if you really want to be adventurous, hire a fishing boat and head for **Güigüi**, the most appealing beach on the island (appealing largely because of its inaccessibility). Fishermen are quite used to requests from tourists wanting to go to Güigüi and will wait to bring you back – but again, strike a mean bargain.

Waiting for a bite

For your return journey it is just as well to take the same road, since to go by any other route entails at least another two hours' drive and dramatic changes in weather conditions as you climb and fall. On the way back, take in **Las Meloneras**, just before Maspalomas with its famous miles of sand dunes, and have a *cubalibre* or *mojito* (rum with crushed lemon) in the bar/restaurant of Santiago before taking a refreshing evening dip.

For an excellent dinner with good service, even better prices and a relaxed atmosphere, I suggest **Loopy's** in **San Agustín** where you can either try the closed pizzas – *calzone* – or the delicious and generous *pinchos* (kebabs) served Loopy-style. Dress up if you want to have a quick flutter at the casino in the **Hotel Tamarindos**. If

On the lonely strand at Güigüi

Canary wrestling

pleasure, you may prefer just to visit the stately animals – all 50 of them.

Back on the road, a little further on, you will see a signpost indicating **Las Lagunas** on the left. Follow this road to visit the **Posada Mirador** which offers some of the most breathtaking views of the island to be had from a hotel balcony. In view of the long, dry journey ahead, it's a good idea to take advantage of its pool. The restaurant is also tempting but save yourself for the Parador later; meanwhile have a quick drink and a snack and then get back on the road.

At **Tunte**, a beautiful unspoilt town, drive past the colourfully painted **Bar Guanche** and turn left for Tejeda. The road now becomes seriously serpentine with one bend on top of the other. Look down to your left to see the **Presa de Chira** (reservoir). Follow the signposts for **Los Pechos** which eventually take you up to the right. At 1,980m (6,496ft) this is the highest point on the island. Also known as **Pozo de las Nieves** (the Snow Well) because of a natural well within the military boundaries which is permanently ice-encrusted, this viewpoint affords wonderful photos of sunsets over Mount Teide on Tenerife. Note: fenced-off areas are out-of-bounds for military reasons.

Wind back down to the main road and turn up to the right for the **Parador**, lying just beyond nasty bends. Before lunch, drink an *aperitivo* on the terrace, which overlooks **Roque Nublo** and **El Fraile** (so named because it looks like a friar kneeling to pray). Try a Bitter Kas, which is similar to Campari except non-alcoholic, served with *aceitunas en mojo* (olives in hot sauce). Lunch is served by cheerful waitresses dressed in traditional Canary costume. The *menú del día* always comprises typical Canary dishes and is excellent value for money.

Roques Bentaiga (right) and Nublo

After lunch, continue down to the village of **Tejeda** and follow the road past the **Roque Bentaiga** until you come to a crossroads at **El Montañón**. This is almond-tree country and all kinds of delica-

Evening at Puerto de Mogán

cies are offered at roadside stalls and shops, some of which have signs in English. Buy the delicious, sticky *bienmesabe* (literally 'I taste good'), made of honey, almonds and sugar and an excellent accompaniment to ice cream.

If you prefer an interesting, scenic run home, with no great complications, take the road that runs through **Taidía**, **Santa Lucía,** with its excellent craft shops, where **La Fortaleza**, a restaurant-cum-museum (open Monday to Saturday 9am–5pm), is well worth a visit, on through **Temisas** and down to **Agüimes**. If you have time, you could also take in the **Barranco de Guayadeque** (see Itinerary 5). From **Agüimes**, which has an attractive centre and is the town *par excellence* of the famous wrestlers of *lucha canaria* (something like Japan's sumo wrestling), make your way back via **Vecindario** to the main road and then back south.

More intrepid travellers whose vehicle is sufficiently sturdy should take the route past *las presas* (the dams). The spectacular scenery along the route compensates for the rough terrain. This lonely route runs past three dams and alongside the beautiful **Pinar de Inagua** forest, regaining the beaten track at the tourist-oriented village of **Mogán**.

Stop off at **Puerto de Mogán**, where the international yachting marina harmonises quite well with the old town behind, and have something to eat and drink in the restaurant in the **Club del Mar** complex; a dip in the hotel's open-air Jacuzzi should leave you in fine fettle for the road back to your resort.

Again, the drive back to Playa del Inglés requires caution: the point where the road offers the best views back over Mogán (especially when the sun is setting over the Puerto) lies on the worst bend on the island.

10. Palmitos Park and Maspalomas

This is not so much an itinerary as a round-up of attractions you may want to try when the beach becomes a bore and you've had enough of exploring. It includes camels, horses, parrots, butterflies, golf and go-karts, the famous Maspalomas Dunes, amusements and shopping.

Los Palmitos Park (daily 9am–6pm) is an artificial, subtropical wildlife park up the road past El Tablero (there is a bus service). Its small lakes, exotic trees and plants harbour tropical birds, butterflies and gibbons. One of the stars of the park is an albino gibbon who was born on the premises. For a leisurely visit, allow two hours at least. Parrot shows are organised eight times daily. Although the park is a little chilly first thing in the morning, it is also less busy then and this is really the best time to go. With the admission charge at just under 1,000ptas for adults (half-price for children) it offers good entertainment value. Ask for the guide to the local flora and look out for the cactus called 'mother-in-law's seat' (No 89).

On your way back down the road towards the sea, you will find **El Rancho Verde** on your right. Here you can hire a camel or a horse for a modest price and gain a good view of the surrounding area from its back. If, however, the last thing you want to do is see more wildlife, then make your way a little further down the road where, on the right, you can try your hand at go-kart racing (open 10am–11pm).

For something more refreshing, drop into **Aquasur**, the big aquadrome just across the road from El Rancho Verde. Slide down the great multicoloured plastic tubes, fight against the artificially created waves in one of the swimming pools or merely lounge around on the sidelines.

Aquasur water-slide

Back in Maspalomas the **Maspalomas Golf Course** (18 holes), Avda Africa (tel: 76 25 81), offers more sedate activity. Golf clubs can be hired, if you don't have your own. After you have worked up an appetite, adjourn for lunch in the unforgettable surroundings of the **Oasis Hotel** restaurant in Maspalomas (near the lighthouse). The daily buffet lunch is decently priced and the gardens with their strutting peacocks and waving palm-trees are beautifully landscaped – perfect for an after-lunch snooze.

For sunbathing, you can't find anywhere better than the **dunes** at Maspalomas (providing there are no high winds to lift the sand). They are real sun-traps and very peaceful. This is actually the nudist part of the beach but you can retain your beachwear if you feel so inclined. However, if you would like to experience nudism but are shy, there are special stone rings which will shield you from the scrutiny of unwelcome onlookers. Be warned: if there is a wind, towels etc quickly become buried, so keep a close eye on them if you go for a swim.

Another possibility is **Ocean Park** (10am–6pm), which is located within the complex of Maspalomas Golf. The complex makes a refreshing change from the beach and you can bask in the shade if you have had too much sun. Grab an enormous rubber ring and float along.

Prickly flowers

Afterwards, if you want to get the adrenalin going again after all the lazing around, next door to Ocean Park is the amusement park **Holidayworld** (6pm–1am; closed Monda). For a little over 1,000ptas children and adults alike can brave the big dipper, the big wheel, the pirate ship, the fly-trap and many other white-knuckle rides. There is a good two hours' entertainment to be had here if you like this kind of thing.

The most comprehensive shopping centre in the region of Playa del Inglés and Maspalomas is **Faro 2** (down Alpitours Street). As well as a good range of shops, the complex offers amusement parlours, a post-office, several bureaux de change, newsagents and a number of good, well-priced restaurants (**Food Core 2** is exceptionally good value).

People who just want to relax over a drink or two should head for **Mamas and Papas**, a piano bar which offers views over the dunes, especially pretty at sunset.

The Maspalomas sand dunes

11. Water Sports and Fishing Trips

Ride a sausage, water-ski, learn how to deep-sea dive or fish for a shark – an assortment of watersports.

You will need to organise your day on the water with care. Spanish sailing laws oblige you to hire someone to pilot your boat as well as the boat itself, and although there are lots of people offering this service they don't always give value for money. Try at **Pasito Blanco** (ask at the petrol station or at the bar) to see if anyone will take you out, but make sure they are insured.

If this fails, the Pegasus Club (tel: 15 10 00/73 63 33), beside the Aquamarina complex at **Patalavaca**, offers a day at sea (10am–5pm) with a barbecue lunch and German cakes and pastries in the late afternoon. A mini-bus is also laid on to take you to and fro (tel: 15 10 00 or 73 63 33). The *Pegasus* is a beautiful sailing boat with a pleasant skipper. The price of around 10,000ptas includes membership of the Pegasus club.

If you prefer something more adventurous, try shark-fishing. The best place for chartering your own boat (six people minimum/eight maximum) is **Puerto Rico**, round the far side of the marina. Telephone bookings are not accepted, but they say Tuesday and Friday are less busy. You can choose between two timetables: 9am–3.30pm or 3.30–8pm. If you want to fish it costs from 5,000ptas; if you only want to watch, it costs a bit less.

If you don't mind an organised trip in the company of rather more people, the *Punta Umbría II* at the entrance to the marina offers breakfast, lunch, shark-fishing, coffee and brandy, with a stop at a small cove along the way, for around 3,500ptas (children under 10 half-price), Monday to Wednesday and weekends 11am–4.30pm). The return coach transfer from your resort is included in the price (tel: 76 26 96).

The **Líneas Salmon** ferry runs between Puerto Rico, Mogán and Arguineguin about every half hour. Mogán offers the possibility of a trip on the *Golden Submarine*, which starts from behind the **Club del Mar** complex.

Galleon excursion

Those who prefer to keep their head above water can learn how to sail, wind-surf, dive or water-ski at Puerto Rico. None of these activities can be learned quickly, however, and aren't cheap. The latest craze, the 'water-sausage', for up to six people, provides thrills for around 2,000ptas.

Shopping

There are lots of things to buy as souvenirs of Gran Canaria. Where you buy depends upon what you are after. Shops open at 10am, close between 2–4pm or 4.30pm, and close again around 8pm. Large stores such as **El Corte Inglés**, **Galerías Preciados** and **Zara**, all in the Mesa y López area, never close at lunchtime and others, such as **Maya** (Triana), stay open all day during festivals, for example between Christmas and 6 January.

Not for taking home!

Every new development is designed to make it easier and more pleasureable for you to spend you pesetas. Recent additions include two big new complexes, one on the outskirts on the route North (Las Arenas), the other on the route to the centre (La Ballena), and the pededstrian precincts in Las Canteras.

Items which are representative of Canary culture are found mainly between the **Calle Armas** in Vegueta (see *Itinerary 1*) or in the **Fataga** shops, one of which is in the Pueblo Canario (see also *Itinerary 1*) and the other in the Parque Santa Catalina next to the Tourist Information Bureau. The Calle Armas establishment is especially good for *naifes* (knifes with goathorn handles), which start off at around 6,000ptas. You can also buy *naife* brooches or even earrings. In wood, you can buy miniature replicas of *balcones canarios* (the famous wooden balconies), *arcones* (caskets), elaborately chiselled picture frames and *pilas*, tiny replicas of the filter stone traditionally used to collect water. The musical instruments on offer are *chacaras* (very big castanets), *timples* (very small guitars) and an odd collection of bones hung on goatskin (which works in a similar way to a washboard). In basketry, there are elaborate cane birdcages and typical local hats and baskets of all shapes and sizes. Earthenware includes the famous *ídolos de Tara*, *cachimbas* (clay pipes) and *pintaderas* (clay seals fashioned into brooches).

In the Fataga shops you will also find lace handkerchiefs, placemats and little figures dressed in the various native costumes of the different islands. Shop assistants will pack items so that they can be easily transported in suitcases.

Canary lace

If you want to buy Canary music, visit the music department in the Corte Inglés (Mesa y López). If it is classical music that you want, buy the *Cantos Canarios* by Teobaldo Power or anything by the modern composer Falcón Sanabria. For folk music, the best representatives are **Los Sabandeños**, **Mestisay** or **Los Gofiones**. In more modern music, the **Parranda Cuasquías** and **Los Coquillos** will demonstrate that there is more to Spanish music than Julio Iglesias.

The Mesa y López area is particularly good for clothes, with shops such as **Cortefiel**, **D'roma**, **Mango**, **Prenatal** (for children's clothes) and **Zara** offering a wide range of possibilities to suit all pockets. Shoe shops abound. You will find **Lurueña** and **López** again but also **Don Juan** at the bottom end of the street.

For anything in the way of cameras, computer games, etc, try **Maya** in Triana, which, unlike the other Indian shops where the custom is to haggle, offers reasonable prices with a guarantee. For souvenirs, look out for the gold *pintaderas* or the little gold replicas of Gran Canaria.

Canary tobacco is another popular purchase. Apart from the cigars, either in stacks from **La Palma** or in boxes (**Condal**), both of which can be purchased in the Canteras shops or in the Corte Inglés, the most popular strong tobacco is **Coronas,** but the strongest of the strong is **Kruger** or **Mecánicos**, both of which come without filters and are rough.

Local flowers

For wine, try the malmseys from Lanzarote. **El Grifo is** the best white wine and **Malvasía** the best rosé. As a rule, red wines are not recommended: *Vino del Monte*, which you can buy in local bars in the Tafira and La Atalaya areas, is an acquired taste.

If you liked them when you tried them, take home some *gofio* and *turrón*, on sale in all the supermarkets. Finally, buy a bouquet of strelitzias to brighten your first days back, or some *drago* seeds, from which you can grow your own magic dragon-tree.

Eating Out

Gran Canaria is very cosmopolitan and many restaurants offer international cuisine along the lines of prawn cocktail, steak and Black Forest gâteau. As such establishments are very easy to find, I have not recommended any of them here: instead I have concentrated on restaurants serving local specialities.

The Canary Islands have a cuisine all of their own. It makes full use of vegetables, which are produced here in abundance, and the many kinds of fish. Local chefs also produce surprisingly good meat dishes, even though meat is usually imported and vacuum-packed. Goat and rabbit – try the succulent *conejo al salmorejo* (rabbit in hot chilli sauce) – are usually local and fresh. Other specialities of the region include *potaje de berros* (water-cress soup) with *gofio* (toasted cornflour), *caldo de pescado* (fish and vegetables with a coriander sauce and *gofio*) and *sancocho* (salt fish with potatoes and sweet potatoes).

Be sure to try the local fish: *cherne* (a kind of bass), *sama*, a type of seabream and *viejas* (not unlike parrotfish), all with *mojo verde*, a herb and garlic sauce, are especially recommended. The cheeses of the region are also magnificent: *queso flor* from Gran Canaria is mild, but if you like strong cheese try the *majorero* (from Fuerteventura). A delicious accompaniment to fish or cheese is *papas arrugadas* (small salty jacket potatoes) served with *mojo picón* (hot chilli sauce).

Vegetarians are well catered for. *Ropa vieja* (literally 'old clothes') is chick-peas with diced potatoes and other vegetables (though be careful, meat is sometimes slipped in too). *Moros y cristianos* (literally, Moors and Christians) is white rice with kidney beans. Salads make full use of fruits: for example, *aguacate* (avocado) and melon are mixed together with papaw and strawberries.

Special today

If you have a sweet tooth, try the *bienmesabe* (a honey and almond confection) and the *turrón* (a kind of nougat).

Eating out is cheap. As with most things, the south is more expensive, in spite of the competition. In the list that follows, $ indicates a meal costing less than 3,000ptas for two, wine included; $$ under 8,000ptas; and $$$ up to 15,000ptas.

Should you feel dubious about trying local food or just feel in need of a change occaisionally, Chinese restaurants abound. One or two Indian restaurants have also opened up, and there are three Japanese establishments. The newest Japanese is beside the bus station at San Telmo and is excellent value for money. A Russian restaurant, **La Balailaika** (Guanarleme) also offers wonderful food at great prices.

Basic ingredients

Canary cuisine

Ca'Cho Damian
León y Castillo, 26, Las Palmas
Tel: 365323
Choose from a tempting array of enormous bowls on the counter or opt for the set menu. Allow staff to advise you on wine.
($$) Visa.

El Herreño
Mendizabal, 5-7, Las Palmas
Tel: 310513
The set menu is usually tempting but if not try a mixture of dishes in *raciones*. Try the *churros de pescado* (fish in batter) and the *carajaca* (liver). Ask for wine from El Hierro: the rosé is the best (*rosado*).
($) No credit cards.

Pepe el Breca
Gumindafe 32, Las Palmas
Tel: 468065
This is the fish restaurant *par excellence*. The best in Canary cuisine. Allow the owners to advise you on what to choose. Book in advance or be prepared to wait with a drink.
($$$) All credit cards accepted.

Pepe el Breca II
Carretera de Fataga, Maspalomas
Tel: 772637
If you didn't make it to the original Pepe el Breca in Las Palmas, don't miss this off-shoot, run by Pepe's daughter, in the south of Gran Canaria. The bass baked in salt is excellent. Typical Canary desserts. Slightly off the beaten track.
($$) All credit cards accepted.

Las Grutas de Artiles
Las Meleguinas s/n, Santa Brígida (Centre)
Tel: 640575/641250
Built into caves 11km (7 miles) outside Las Palmas), the food is typically Canary. Recommended for a romantic night out, but avoid Saturdays, when wedding and first communion parties are invariably installed.
($$) Visa, Master Card.

Fresh fish

Tenderete II
Av S B de Tirajana, Edificio Aloe, Playa del Inglés
Tel: 761460
Nice atmosphere, great food and very good service.
($$) All credit cards accepted.

La Farola
C Alcalá Galiano 3, Puerto de Arinaga
Tel: 180410
Upmarket establishment in the tiny port of Arinaga. Specialises in seafood. Relaxed ambience.
($$$) All credit cards accepted.

Spanish Food (Regional)

Amaiur
Pérez Galdós, 2, Las Palmas
Tel: 370717
Imaginative dishes from the Basque country, one of the greatest gastronomic regions of Spain. Expect to rub shoulders with local politicians since the restaurant lies across the road from the Government offices in San Bernardo.
($$$) American Express, Diners, Master Card, Visa.

El Padrino
J.Nazareno, 1, Las Coloradas
Las Palmas
Tel: 272094
Seafood.
Fresh fish served in pleasant out-of-town surroundings with fine views over Las Cánteras. Especially recommended is *parrillada de pescado*, an enormous dish of grilled fish of all varieties, washed down with the white wine El Grifo from Lanzarote (*semiseco* – medium dry).
($$) All credit cards accepted.

Canguro
C Travieso 27, Las Palmas
Tel: 366002
and
C Venegas 23, Las Palmas
Tel: 366740
Both restaurants are recognisable by a wooden kangaroo at the door. Though they are in the same area, the one in C Travieso (off Triana) is the quieter of the two. Food is well-

Cave restaurant, Barranco de Guayadeque

priced and inventive. In particular, look out for the spinach with pine kernels and raisins (*espinacas a la Catalena*) and the excellent fish which goes under the unpromising name of *burro* (donkey).
($$) Visa.

Don Quijote
S Artiles 74, Las Palmas
Tel: 272786
Great Fondues, crêpes and *carne a la piedra* – stone-grilled meats you cook yourself. The wine on the table – as opposed to the table wine – can usually be recommended.
($$) Visa.

El Secuestro
Teror (centre)
Grilled meat, succulent *chorizo* and black puddings (*morcillas*) from Teror. Not for small appetites. The atmosphere is rustic. Always crowded on Sunday and holidays.
($) Closed Monday. No credit cards.

L'Orangerie
Av del Oasis s/n
Hotel Maspalomas Palm Beach (South)
Tel: 762924
The menu changes every day according to the fish and vegetables is in season. Elegant restaurant serving excellent food.
($$$) All credit cards accepted.

Rias Bajas
Edificio Playa Sol, Av de Tirajana, Playa del Inglés
Tel: 764033
This restaurant specialises in Galician cuisine, so seafood is a must. In particular, t`ry the *empanada* (a kind of vegetable and tuna pie) and the *tarta de Santiago* (almond cake). Be guided by the chef.
($$) Visa, American Express.

Buffet spread

Other Cuisines

La Pasta Real
Secretario Padilla, 28, Las Palmas
Tel: 262267
Italian and macrobiotic.
The owner used to work in the Scottish town of St Andrew's and therefore speaks fluent English with a broad Scots accent. Service is excellent. The menu, chalked up on a blackboard, includes so many delicious dishes you will probably want to return.
($) Visa, Diners.

Le Français
Sargento Llagas, 18, Las Palmas
Tel: 266762
Wonderful food from the great gastronomic regions of France. The desserts are mouthwatering.
($$) Visa, American Express.

Seafood paella

Nightlife

Possibly one of the reasons for the Canary Islander's famous *aplatanamiento* (literally the 'state of becoming a banana') is that they love to stay out until all hours, dancing and making merry. If you decide to drop in on any of the special events, you will see how people go all out to have a good time even in the smallest village. Of course, the bigger the festivity, the more elaborate the celebration, but you can always count on finding *papagüevos* (giants on stilts or enormous-headed dwarves), a firework display and a *verbena*, a shindig in the village square with rollicking live music supplied by the local band. (Look out for the old faithfuls of the popular Banda de Agaete, an essential ingredient in any good celebration on Gran Canaria.)

The best thing about these celebrations is their community spirit. Apart from during the very few slow dances, everyone dances with everyone else, regardless of age or any other differences. People usually drink beer or *cubalibre* at these events and no celebration is complete without the *tollos* and *pejines* (two kinds of salty fish with a texture like chewing-gum, guaranteed to give you a healthy thirst). This and Carnival are the only occasions when you are expected to pay as you drink. Note: a waistpouch is wise since handbags are cumbersome and wallets in danger.

If you are looking for something more sophisticated in the way of nightlife, then Gran Canaria is the place for you also. But be warned on two counts: nobody who has any pretensions to being cool goes out before midnight, and discos exist primarily for facilitating brief encounters with the opposite sex (in some cases women are admitted free to encourage their custom). The locals are not backward at coming forward and are always keen to practise their language skills – especially since the level of decibels in discos usually makes close proximity essential. The music to dance to at the moment is *bakalao* and the in crowd do

a circuit known as *la ruta del bakalao* (literally the 'cod route'), which winds up in **La Roca** in San Agustín, in the south of the island (the less energetic can drop into **La Quinta Avenida**, next door to La Roca).

As with shops (see *Shopping, pages 62–3*), different areas offer different varieties of nightlife. In Las Palmas, in the area towards Vegueta and behind Triana (around Teatro Pérez Galdós), the bars are more restrained in style, designed for an 'older' young generation. This is totally in keeping with the general atmosphere of the area, which is more relaxed and refined. Begin your evening here at around 11pm (take a taxi to the theatre), perhaps kicking off with **Pool** in the Calle San Pedro, behind the theatre, which offers live music, a pool table (as the name indicates) and pleasant company. **Yurfa** is another old favourite. Housed in an old Canary building in Calle Perdomo, this bar provides good music, art exhibitions, excellent prices and lots of quiet corners where you can sit down and talk without straining the vocal chords.

Glitz at Pachá

After midnight, the place to head is the **Plaza de la Victoria**, with its many noisy, bustling bars. Again, take a taxi. The neighbours who live above the pubs don't take kindly to spirited revellers so you are advised to stand under the protection of the awnings: more than one irate local has been known to 'water' the clientele gathered below.

Heineken is the golden-oldie of these tiny bars. The jukebox music is also mainly golden oldies. However, the latest place to be is **El Cinco**, another terraced bar in Plaza de la Victoria. If your idea of an enjoyable night on the town includes male strippers or wet T-shirts on Schwarzenegger lookalikes you may want to try **La Geiser** next door. Alternatively, ask the taxi driver to take you to the Calle Isla de Cuba. The new bar on the corner, **La Pila,** is currently the most popular, and right next door is an old favourite, **La Tienda**. Cheap and cheerful, this is frequented by the less pretentious Canary youth. One street behind in Ruiz de Alda, is **El Pickup**, currently very popular.

Around 2am, you should be thinking of making a move towards El Puerto, which you can walk to quite easily from Calle Isla de Cuba. If you are looking for glitz and glitter, then **Pachá**, behind the Saba car park and down on the harbour front, is the place to go. If you are feeling energetic, squeeze onto its tiny dance floor in front of a giant video screen, or have a relatively quiet drink

Bar Heineken

on the outside terrace.

Outside terraces spring up like mushrooms in the summer/autumn months. **La Latina** in the marina and **Varadero**, beside the jetfoil station, along by the harbour, are where the beautiful people hang out.

If you are looking for something a little more informal in the jeans line, **Toca-Toca** in the Secretario Artiles is extremely lively at weekends as is its neighbour, **Area**, a disco/bar where they play only Spanish music. The perennially popular **Diseño** in Nicolás Estévanez and **Utopía** in Tomás Miller have maintained their appeal over the years by constantly revising their image. Both venues are always very loud and crowded.

If your tastes in music and nightlife are more sedate, adjourn to the piano-bar **La Clave,** in Alfredo Jones, which allows singalongs. And if you want to try your hand (and feet) at dancing *sevillanas* and flamenco, try the **Sala Rociero** in the Calle Olof Palme, just round the corner from Plaza de la Victoria. Karaoke clubs/bars have also sprung up around this area.

For those with an insatiable need to party, **Cuperón** opens when all the other bars close (at 6am) and offers good music right through until midday.

Down South, where you go depends pretty much on which resort you are staying in, but generally speaking every shopping centre (except Faro 2) has one or two places which are the in-places for the area, where locals come to to sit on the terrace and watch the passing crowds. These change from one year to the next so you must play it by ear – literally. Recently, however, the Kasbah's biggest pulls are **El Garaje** and **Fantasy Island** whilst in the Plaza shopping centre in Maspalomas it is **Pachá** and **Chic.** People who like to bop until they drop should try **La Roca** (San Agustín), strictly for those with stamina.

If your taste in nightlife runs to caberet, try **Son Amor** at the Meliá Tamarindos Hotel in San Augustín, which offers spectacular Las Vegas-style shows. This hotel also has a **casino** offering roulette, blackjack, chemin du fer, baccarat, and slot machines (men are required to wear a tie and everyone is required to show their passport or identity card to get in).

Hot but cool

Calendar of Special Events

It is hardly an exaggeration to say that every day is a *fiesta* in Gran Canaria. Celebration of name days, religious feast days, local historical events and ancient traditions are frequent. Rare is the day when fireworks are not going off somewhere round the island.

Like everything else in Gran Canaria, the local festivities are a peculiar mixture of pagan revelry and Christian solemnity. Celebrations common to the whole of the island may include organised competitions of *lucha canaria* (the traditional Canary wrestling) or even displays of local dancing and singing.

If you attend a fiesta, you'll need plenty of energy. If a celebration begins mid-morning, it is usual to continue partying until the small hours of the next day. The Canary Islanders take their revelry seriously. Carnival, for example, a sleepless seven-day event, rivals the one in Río de Janeiro.

JANUARY

New Year is a major event. People celebrate either at home, on the beach with fireworks or in a nightclub or disco where *collones* (special festivities complete with party hats, streamers and silly plastic noses) are organised. Whichever way, tradition insists that revellers swallow 12 grapes, chime by chime, for good luck, plus lots of *cava* (sparkling wine).

On the 5th islanders buy presents for **Día de Reyes** (the Day of the Three Wise Men) which falls on the 6th. On the evening of the 5th every village and town holds a procession of the Three Wise Men. As the processions are held at different times, it is pos-

Fiesta dress

sible to see up to nine Wise Men on a variety of mounts (camels, donkeys or horses) or even motorised. The 6th is a national holiday though restaurants stay open.

FEBRUARY

The main celebration is **Carnival**, usually the last week of February and the first week of March, though different parts of the island begin and end at different times, beginning in Agüimes and ending in Maspalomas. Look out for the competition of the **Murgas**, bands of singers who poke fun at local politicians and events; the **Elección de la Reina**, the Carnival Queen contest awash in sequins and feathers; the **Fiesta de la Sábana**, the Sheet Party, where all you need is a sheet and imagination; the different *mogollones*, open air dances with *salsa* music; the Carnival Parade and the **Entierro de la Sardina**, the Burial of the Sardine followed by the Widows' Dance, possibly the best part of the whole Carnival.

MARCH/APRIL

After a month of pagan revelry, 19 March is the Feast of **San José** (St Joseph, and thus Father's Day). Since the Spaniards celebrate their name day, this is one of the most important days of the year.

Semana Santa (the dates change every year), most famous for the celebrations at Seville, is also taken very seriously in Gran Canaria, with everything closed on Holy Thursday and Good Friday. Processions abound in all parts of Gran Canaria. 29 April marks the controversial celebration of the Spanish **Conquest.**

MAY

1 May is Labour Day (**Día del Trabajo**) with the traditional demonstrations of the trade unions. The 30th is the **Día de Canarias**, an official holiday celebrated throughout the Canary Islands to mark the anniversary of the granting of autonomous rule to the archipelago.

Carnival revellers

JUNE

17 June is the feast day of **Corpus Christi** when streets of various towns and Vegueta in Las Palmas are painstakingly covered with carpets of flowers. The 24th marks the feast of **San Juan**, doubly important since it is also the anniversary of the founding of the city of Las Palmas. A whole week of events is organised, including open-air concerts and folklore. On the night of San Juan, which is the Spaniards' equivalent of Hallowe'en, bonfires are built, especially on the beaches.

JULY

The 16th marks the celebrations of the **Fiestas del Carmen**, patron saint of all those who work on the seas and greatly revered by the Canary islanders. The most moving processions are held in the Puerto de la Luz, La Isleta, Gáldar and Mogán. From the 22–25 July, the most important celebrations for Gáldar and San Bartolomé de Tirajana take place, the **Fiestas de Santiago el Apóstol**.

AUGUST

The other great traditional pagan celebration is held on 4 August: **La Bajada de la Rama** in Agaete. This celebrates one of the rain-making rituals of the *Canarios*. The 29th is the celebration of the **Virgen de la Cuevita** in Artenara, marked by a torch-lit night procession.

SEPTEMBER

Possibly the biggest celebration on Gran Canaria is held on 8 September, the **Virgen del Pino** in Teror. The locals make a night pilgrimage to Teror, some of them proceeding on their knees. The 10 September

Religious procession

marks another typical *Canarios'* celebration, the **Fiesta del Charco** in San Nicolás de Tolentino where the locals fish with their hands in a specially rigged pool.

OCTOBER

The **Fiestas de la Naval** are celebrated in La Isleta and the area called La Naval, around 6 October. They celebrate the victory over Sir Francis Drake in 1595. National festivities, consisting mainly of military parades, of the **Día de la Hispanidad** take place on the 12th.

NOVEMBER/DECEMBER

1 November is **Día de los Difuntos** (All Souls' Day). 6 December is the **Día de la Constitución** (to celebrate the Constitution on which democratic Spain is based), not usually an official holiday. The 25th, of course, is **Christmas** when you should look out for the *belenes* (nativities) in San Gregorio, Telde, in the Museo de Piedras, Ingenio and the 'live' nativity staged in Agaete.

Practical Information

Inter-island transport

GETTING THERE

The usual way to reach Gran Canaria is by plane – though you can always opt for the combination of flying to Tenerife, to the Reina Sofía airport and then taking a taxi up to Santa Cruz where you can catch the Jetfoil directly to Las Palmas de Gran Canaria. The Jetfoil service runs a winter and a summer timetable. To find out when there is a jetfoil available (the travelling time is 1hour, 40 minutes), phone Trasmediterránea, tel: (928) 265650.

There are lots of charter flights to Gran Canaria. Although it is possible to find flight only deals, it usually works out cheaper to take a package with accommodation included.

The airport at Gandó in Gran Canaria is in the process of being extended to accommodate not only tourists to this island but also those travelling on to Lanzarote or Fuerteventura. If you are travelling under your own steam, you can either take the airport bus to the centre of Las Palmas de Gran Canaria (around 500ptas) or catch a taxi, which will charge a standard price of around 2,000ptas. To travel down south if you are not on a package trip is expensive. Although a regular bus service does exist, it leaves from the far side of the very busy motorway – not the airport itself – and there is no bridge to help you get across. Taxis charge 4,000–5,000ptas for the run to Playa del Inglés. If you are going further than that, ask for a quote first.

TRAVEL ESSENTIALS

When to Go

High season (*temporada alta*) begins in October and runs through to April/May. Although it is true to say that Gran Canaria has sun and even temperatures all year round, the best months are September and October, when schools restart in Spain. The south enjoys sunshine all year round, which is why many tour operators have introduced sunshine guarantee clauses in their holiday offers. However, although the weather is beautifully warm in Jan-

Year-round sun

uary and February, the water itself is icy cold.

July and August are months to be avoided if possible since this is when the locals are on holiday themselves and everything is much more crowded. It is also when Las Palmas de Gran Canaria is victim of the *panza de burro* (see *Climate*) which produces intense heat but little real sunshine.

Climate

The average temperature in Gran Canaria is 22°C (72°F) although, as I point out throughout this guidebook, the temperature varies according to the altitude. The south in general is rarely overcast, though on the days when there is *viento del sur*, a kind of sirocco, the sky is a dull grey. It is a mistake to think you are quite safe from sunburn on these days, for the ultra-violet rays are trapped between the leaden sky and the beach, producing what the locals call *resol*, 'double sun'.

When the day is windy, the locals avoid the Playa del Inglés and Maspalomas and make for beaches further west, such as Puerto Rico and Taurito, which are more sheltered.

In Las Palmas de Gran Canaria, the *sirocco* brings sand from Morocco, producing a very disagreeable thunderous atmosphere (*polvo en suspensión* – literally 'dust in the air'). People who suffer from allergies should try to head south when this occurs since to stay in the city until the rain rinses away the problem can mean a great deal of suffering. When it rains, it rains hard, but only in very short bursts and the temperature remains the same. March and April are the months when the weather is most unsettled, but even then this affects only the higher regions of the island.

Year-round swimming

Two other phenomena which you should be aware of are the famous *panza de burro* or 'donkey's belly', an enormous grey cloud which settles over the capital of the island in July/August, producing intense heat, and the *mar de nubes* (or 'sea of clouds'). You can climb up above the clouds but any hopes of taking panoramic photographs of the island are ruined. However, neither of these phenomena tend to last more than one day at a time. Rolling mists (and they travel at speed) can also be found on higher ground.

Clothing

Coats and jackets are not needed but a light cardigan or pullover is necessary if you are intending to travel up to higher regions. Sunglasses are a must and a pair of plastic sandals for use on some of the beaches is a good idea since there may be rocks underfoot.

Sensible footwear is necessary if you are thinking of walking around to any great extent and some kind of head protection is also important. Men should take a tie if they intend visiting the casino. Umbrellas are not worth packing; in the rare case of needing one, you will find they are sold dirt cheap in the Corte Inglés in Las Palmas.

Documents

You need a valid passport and an international driving licence if you plan on hiring a car. You should also take out some kind of travel insurance to safeguard against accidents and pick up the E111 form from your local post office before leaving home; this entitles EU citizens to free medical treatment.

A religious mix

Electricity

The electricity supply is 220 volts, and the Spaniards use round two-pin sockets, so UK visitors will need an adaptor for any electrical appliances. Four-star and five-star hotels provide hairdriers. Laundry services are cheap and often preferable to the results of a travel iron.

Time Differences

There is an hour's difference between mainland Spain and the Canary Islands. Gran Canaria is usually on the same time as Great Britain but when the clocks change there may be a week or so when there are two hours' difference.

GETTING ACQUAINTED

Geography

The Canary archipelago is on latitude 28° and comprises seven inhabited islands, an eighth which is partially inhabited (La Graciosa), four or five uninhabited islands (Lobos, Montaña Clara, Alegranza, Roque del Este, Roque del Oeste) and another mythical island, San Borondón (St Brendan's), which appears and disappears at will.

The seven islands are divided between two provinces: Las Palmas which includes Gran Canaria, Fuerteventura, Lanzarote, La Graciosa (and the uninhabited islands) and Tenerife which takes in Tenerife, La Palma, El Hierro and La Gomera.

People in Gran Canaria are very touchy about visitors confusing them with the Balearic Islands or with Tenerife.

Government and Economy

The Canary Islands have an autonomous regional government with fully devolved powers in very limited fields. The economy, which was formerly dependent upon agriculture, began to rely heavily on tourism in the 1960s. This industry now represents almost 80 percent of the archipelago's total income.

At times, the Canary islanders have protested that the central government in Spain is insensitive to their situation as isolated islands. Since most products are imported, the cost of living is high compared with the rest of Spain. With full integration of Spain and the Canary Islands in the EU, locals believe that their cost of living will suffer.

Parties of a nationalist nature have sprung up over the last few years. One of these in particular, ATI, has had so much success that it holds the balance of power in a regional coalition government with the Socialist party, PSOE.

Population and Religion

There is a great ethnic mix in Gran Canaria. People from all parts of the world have come here for business or pleasure and stayed to become fully integrated in society. Thus all religions have been represented here for some time. The Templo Ecuménico in the south holds multilingual religious ceremonies. There is also a mosque in the Yumbo shopping centre in the south and various churches of the Latter-Day Saints scattered over the island.

MONEY MATTERS

It is best to come with peseta traveller's cheques and local currency. Money changers are many and their rates differ widely. Avoid *bureaux de change* in hotels if possible, for they tend to offer poor rates. Always try to change money in banks (open from 9am–2pm, closed Saturday).

Some banks have currency exchange points (eg Caja de Madrid in Calle Albareda) similar to cash machines outside their premises. These are not recommended except when all other options are closed.

Credit cards are widely accepted, above all American Express and Visa. Cash points in the area of El Puerto are usually housed inside booths, for obvious reasons, and allow you to carry out your transactions in the language of your choice.

Remember that the harbour area suffers from all the typical problems of such a district, so do not display money or valuables and don't carry wallets in back pockets. A money belt or a pouch are wise investments.

Tipping

Perhaps expected in restaurants and hairdressers but not elsewhere. Ten percent is the norm.

GETTING AROUND

Las Palmas de Gran Canaria with over 350,000 inhabitants is almost worse to drive in than London. People use their cars for absolutely everything and want to park right next to their destination. Since the city was originally planned for a small number of vehicles and it is estimated that there is an average of at least two cars per person of driving age in the capital, the effect is bedlam. For inner-city travel I suggest you use the *guaguas* (buses), which are cheap (75ptas) and cheerful. A *bono guagua* (pronounced boneoh wawa) which can be used for 10 journeys costs 500ptas and can be bought in any bank.

Taxis are good value with the longest run in the city costing only around 300ptas. Walking is only pleasant in Las Palmas in pedestrian areas such as Vegueta, the Avda Marítima or around Las Canteras.

To travel around the island you can use the green buses, the SALCAI (tel: 36 88 31 for information), which run a particularly fast line down to the south, or the UTINSA (tel: 37 36 25) which tend to be slower and serve rural areas. Both services leave from the bus station across from the Parque San Telmo.

However, the easiest way to travel round the island is by car, especially since the introduction of colourful new signposting. You can hire anything from a Seat Panda (approximately 2,000ptas per day) to a Mitsubishi mini-van which costs around 10,000ptas a day and seats nine. Rates are much the same at all companies, but Avis, Betacar and Autos Moreno offer the most reliable service. There is a larger variety of vehicles to choose from outside the airport.

For organised excursions, Tamaragua (tel: 27 20 00) in Nicolás Estévanez and in the south, or any of the branches of Ultramar Express (tel: 27 30 22) offer you everything from shark-fishing to belly-dancing at competitive prices.

To travel between the islands, the Jetfoil serves Fuerteventura and Tenerife (tel: 26 56 50) and ferries which take cars serve all the islands. There is an excellent inter-island flight service (tel: 57 42 20/25 41 40 for information), but remember that flights are heavily booked at Christmas, Easter and in July/August. Book in any travel agency.

Winding roads

Idyllic anchorage

HOURS & HOLIDAYS

The people in the Canary Islands work according to two timetables: one for the so-called summer and the other for the rest of the year. Most of the time, life is geared to schedules on mainland Spain. Schools start at 8–8.30am (take note if your hotel/apartment is near a school), but there are so many children of school age (although the birthrate in the Canary Islands has fallen) that high school students are taught in shifts and may still be at their desks at 8pm.

Offices are supposed to open at about 9am but few make it before 9.30, apart from the banks, some of which begin at 8.30am. Shops open around 10am, which is the time El Corte Inglés opens, although food shops are open earlier. They close again at 2pm and reopen around 4pm. Everything closes around 8pm though you will find places in Las Canteras which stay open later.

The summer timetable is applied by offices such as the Tourist Information Office, in the months of July and August, due to lack of staff. In those months offices open from 9am–2pm and do not reopen in the afternoon.

The people of Gran Canaria do not take a *siesta*. In fact, they do not appear to sleep very much at all, which possibly explains the slow rhythm all through the day. Nightlife rarely begins until around midnight and continues well into the morning.

Taxis are available 24 hours a day and the airport is also open all night.

Remember that public holidays (see *Calendar of Special Events*) are kept religiously – only restaurants and some bars do not close. If the holiday falls on a Thursday, Friday is also taken as a holiday. People all over Spain are experts at inventing *puentes*, ie long weekends.

ACCOMMODATION

Generally speaking, the accommodation in the south of the island is of excellent standard and offers possibilities for all pockets. Las Palmas de Gran Canaria tends to cater more for business people than for tourists *per se* and accommodation divides between the very good and the very bad with little in between. Since people no longer tend to stay the whole time in Las Palmas but go south for the sunshine, lots of the hotels have become rather rundown.

In the capital, the best hotels cost around 12,000ptas per night whilst more modest, yet decent accommodation costs around 4,000ptas per night. In the following recommendations *$* indicates accommodation under 5,000 ptas, *$$* is under 20,000ptas, and *$$$* over 20,000ptas. All price guides are for a double room.

Hotel Santa Catalina (tel: 243040, *$$$*) is possibly the most expensive of the hotels in Las Palmas, clocking in at around 20,000ptas per night, but worth it. On **Las Canteras** itself, however, there is a wide choice to suit all tastes. **Hotel Imperial Playa** (tel: 264854, *$$*) which belongs to the NH chain is, like most, a refurbished old hotel with wonderful views and magnificent rooms. **Hotel Meliá** (tel: 267600, *$$*), **Reina Isabel** (tel: 260100, *$$*) and the **Hotel Sansofé** (tel: 224062, *$$*) are also on the beachfront. Hotel Sansofé should be given a miss if it only has back rooms available since the hotel borders on the seedier side of Las Canteras and the back streets are active, in all senses.

Should you want something cheaper and yet still decent, try **Hotel Cantur** (tel: 262304, *$*), a little back from the beachfront but still on Las Canteras, or **Hotel**

Atlanta (tel: 265062, $) behind the Reina Isabel in Calle Alfredo Jones. Clocking in at the same price, and possibly the best bet if you want to do your own thing, are the apartments **Colón Playa** (tel: 265954, $) on the beachfront at the end of Alfredo Jones, which offer seaviews and a central position.

Down south, you can choose between different resorts and different types of accommodation. In San Agustín, favoured by islanders, **Hotel Gloria Palace** (tel: 768300, $$), built largely for congresses, is new, well-laid out and exceptionally comfortable. In Playa del Inglés, **Hotel Parque Tropical** (tel: 760712, $$) is beautifully designed, central and decently priced as well as being the place where local and international stars stay when appearing at the nightclub Don Gato next door.

The best hotel if you are staying in Maspalomas is the **Oasis**, with double rooms either looking onto the Oasis or onto the sea. Either way, the view is beautiful. Rooms here costs around 20,000ptas for a double. Patalavaca, just round the corner from Arguineguín, offers the **Steigenberg Canaria** (tel: 150400, $$) with incredible sunset vistas. In Mogán the beautiful **Club de Mar** complex (little Venice) costs a very decent 10,000ptas (tel: 740100, $$).

However, as I said, you can find apartments and bungalows to suit all pockets. Consult the travel agencies mentioned in *Getting Around* or in El Corte Inglés.

Camping is another option, but sites tend to be noisy (everybody takes their TV), crowded and with few facilities. They are good for meeting people, however, and for travellers on shoestring budgets. (Information from the campsites at Pasito Blanco and Taurito.)

CULTURAL EVENTS

The Canary islanders have always felt culturally disadvantaged compared with their fellow countrymen, though very unnecessarily so. Consequently a great deal of effort is made to compensate. An esteemed International Festival of Classical Music is held every February (tickets and programmes from SOCAEM well in advance to avoid disappointment; tel: 291944/ 292588). There are also festivals of opera, light opera (*zarzuela*) – details from SOCAEM also – and ballet, and travelling theatre groups regularly appear at the Teatro Pérez Galdós. The University of Las Palmas de Gran Canaria organises various courses throughout the year (see newspapers for details) and a summer school every August, with speakers from all parts of the world. The CAAM also organises excellent seminars to coincide with their exhibitions.

HEALTH & EMERGENCIES

Should you need attention for anything more serious than insect bites, sunburn or a gippy stomach, you should make for the emergency services (*Urgencias*) in any of the following hospitals: Clínica del Pino in the Calle Tomás Morales (tel: 23 11 99), the Materno-Infantil (principally maternity and children's hospital but attends all kinds of cases and ages), Avda Marítima del Sur (tel: 32 03 33) or the Hospital Insular, also in the Avda Marítima (tel: 31 30 33), in Las Palmas de Gran Canaria. These are the hospitals which look after the general population. There are usually English-speaking doctors and nurses around, but if you need to explain your problem without misunderstanding of any kind, then your best bet is to make for the Hospital Inglés, Paseo de la Cornisa, 1 (tel: 25 42 43) which, as its name indicates, has English-speaking staff.

Do not drink the water from the tap under any circumstances. Try to avoid it even for brushing your teeth and eschew ice in your drinks. Bottled water comes in two types, *con* (with) or *sin* (without) *gas*, so you do not have to drink the bubbly if you don't want to. Buy this in supermarkets as bars inflate prices. Should you be caught by a dose of diarrhoea, ask for Fortasec in the chemist's and avoid drinking alcohol for at least six hours. One tablet does the trick.

Although it is immensely difficult, try to avoid over-exposure to the sun. Keep out of direct sunlight from 1–4pm and watch out for kids catching double dosage in the water. Acute sunburn or sunstroke should be treated in a hospital (Clínica Scandinavica (tel: 771638) or the Suomi British Clinic (tel: 762742) both in the south).

Crime

The people of Gran Canaria are still peaceful and law-abiding but, as happens in any big city with a busy harbour area, there are problems, especially bag-snatching and theft. Do not court trouble and only carry your passport and other papers around when absolutely necessary, ie when changing money. In Las Palmas, the area beyond and behind the Sansofé hotel is not particularly safe at night and is perfectly easy to avoid. The same can be said of Ripoche.

The south is not free from these problems either, especially its bungalows, which are less well protected. Should you have problems contact the nearest *comisaría* (police station). Sometimes, you may need to ask your consulate for help, as not all police stations have interpreting services. For emergencies of any kind, dial 091.

Typical tiling

SPORT

The south of the island is the place for water sports, with lessons in water-skiing, diving, underwater fishing, windsurfing and sailing all on offer for those who have time to learn. The best place for these, and for shark fishing, is Puerto Rico.

If you want to go your own way and don't need tuition then Pozo Izquierdo is the best place for windsurfing (signposted on the road down to the south, around Arinaga). The world championship heats were held here only recently. Playa del Aguila, just before San Agustín and Bahía Feliz are also good for windsurfing. For ordinary surfers, the area around Bañaderos and the end of the Canteras beach, beside the road out to the north, are the best places.

Vela latina (a highly skilful type of sailing) is not easy to understand but very popular with the natives (the sport generates a lot of betting). *Lucha canaria* may be programmed to celebrate special events and is very exciting to watch – as are the *lucha del garrote* (*juego del garrote*) competitions.

There is a golf course at Maspalomas (see *Itinerary 10*) and Bandama (*see Itinerary 3*). The football season begins in September – but visiting spectators should avoid matches between U D Las Palmas and Tenerife, which are well known for their violence.

MAPS

Pick up the excellent freebies in El Corte Inglés in Las Palmas. The Tourist Information office (Parque Santa Catalina) can also provide you with detailed maps.

TOILETS

Unlike on mainland Spain, toilets in bars and restaurants are generally well-tended. Don't use the toilets in the Parque Santa Catalina, however, or any other public toilet. Agaete doesn't win the award for Gran Canaria's most scrupulous town on this account.

Lack of toilets is one of the handicaps of Carnival merrymaking. The portable loos provided are grossly insufficient. Your best option is to pop into a bar – nobody will object.

COMMUNICATIONS & NEWS

For long-distance phone calls I suggest you use telephone booths or exchanges. If you can avoid it, don't phone from hotels, since the mark-up is steep. The prefix for Tenerife and province is 922. The prefix for Gran Canaria is 928. You don't need to use it within the island nor for Lanzarote or Fuerteventura. To dial other countries (Canada follows the US system) first dial the international access code 07, then the country code: Australia (61); France (33); Germany (49); Italy (39); Japan (81); Netherlands (31); UK (44); US (1).

If using a US credit phone card, dial the company's access number below. Sprint, Tel: 900 99 0013; AT&T, Tel: 900 99 00 11; MCI, Tel: 900 99 0014.

Gran Canaria has three newspapers – *Canarias 7*, *La Provincia* and *Diario de Las Palmas*. All major European daily newspapers are on the news stands the day following publication.

USEFUL ADDRESSES

Tourist Information

Spanish National Tourist Office
57–58 St James' Street
London SW1
Tel: (0171) 499 4593/499 3257

Oficina de Turismo
Parque Santa Catalina, Las Palmas
Tel: 277356

Consulates

France
Calle Néstor de la Torre, 12
Tel: 244012

Germany
Calle José Franchy y Roca, 5
Tel: 275700

United Kingdom
Calle Luis Morote, 6
Tel: 262508

United States
Calle José Franchy y Roca, 5–5°
Tel: 271259

FURTHER READING

Insight Guide: Gran Canaria, Lanzarote and Fuerteventura (Apa Publications 1990, updated 1995), provides excellent background reading as well as information on all the sights and a comprehensive travel tips section.

If you are interested in exploring the island by foot, the Sunflower Countryside Guide, *Landscapes of Gran Canaria* by Noel Rochford, provides a sensible and comprehensive selection of walking tours, some of which form part of the Tourist Board's new project to restore the *caminos reales* (royal routes) which linked towns before the island's roads were developed. For culture vultures, the CAAM (El Centro Atlantico de Arte Moderno) publishes all its catalogues in bilingual (English/Spanish) editions.

Sunset over Roque Nublo, with Tenerife's Mt Teide in the distance

Index

A

B

C

M

N, O

P

R

S

Art & Photo Credits

Photography **Paul Young** *and*
Pages 10, 11, 12, 13, 14T, 34T, 47T, 74 **Andrew Eames**
5B, 26, 33, 80 **Wolfgang Fritz**
25, 66T, 72 **Tulio Gatti**
35, 53T, 64, 67B, 68, 75B, 76, 77B, 78 **Roger Hilton**
66 **Sergio Rodriguez Matos**
27, 38, 61 **Gary John Norman**
59T, 63B, 65, 79 **Nigel Tisdall**
71 **Bill Wassman**

Handwriting **V. Barl**
Production Editor **Erich Meyer**
Cover Design **Klaus Geisler**
Cartography **Berndtson & Berndtson**